RIDE ALONG WITH CHICAGO'S FINEST IN THE CITY THAT WORKS

"Turn off CSI and see what police-work is really about. Daniel Smith has successfully opened the door to the private entrance of the Chicago Police Department. On the Job *is an emotional and heartfelt journey inside one of America's oldest and most respected police departments. This story is one that only a member of the family could tell."*

—Lee Lofland, author of *The Book of Police Procedure and Investigation* (2007)

"In a cop's world, the one truth is making it through your tour of duty alive—everything else is just a matter of interpretation. Armed only with an unflinching eye, Danny Smith invades that world to discover the truths, examine the shadows, and interpret the culture of those who hold the line. A must-read for anyone interested in the real story behind the blue."

—Gina Gallo, author of *Armed and Dangerous: Memoirs of a Chicago Policewoman*

"On the Job is an excellent and much needed addition to the literature on the Chicago Police Department. With this study, Daniel P. Smith provides an insightful and thought-provoking look at those beneath the star, the challenges of the profession, and the remarkable city these officers call home."

—Frank Kusch, author of *Battleground Chicago: The Police and the 1968 Democratic National Convention*

"Told with sensitivity and candor, On the Job: Behind the Stars of the Chicago Police Department *is both inspiring and tragic. The story of everyday police officers serving on the front lines reveals the human side of 'the job.' Mr. Smith has weaved a fine narrative on the inner workings of a secret, oath-bound brotherhood, the impact of this 'job' upon their personal lives, and what it really means to be one of 'Chicago's Finest.'"*

—Richard C. Lindberg, Chicago historian and the author of *To Serve and Collect: Chicago Politics and Police Corruption from the Lager Beer Riot to the Summerdale Scandal, 1855-1960*

*"*On the Job *tells the real story of Chicago Police. Chicago is like a small town in which Smith, because of his own background and credentials, was able to get cops to share their stories, which are too little told. Here is an honest dialogue which those of us who care about this city and others are privileged to read.* On the Job *fills an important gap in our oral history as a city and as a people."*

—Dick Simpson, Head of the Department of Political Science University of Illinois at Chicago and former Chicago Alderman

On the Job

Behind the Stars
of the
Chicago Police
Department

By Daniel P. Smith

First Edition

LAKE CLAREMONT PRESS
www.lakeclaremont.com
Chicago

On the Job:
Behind the Stars of the Chicago Police Department

Daniel P. Smith

Published February 2008 by:

lcp@lakeclaremont.com
www.lakeclaremont.com

Publisher's Cataloging-In-Publication Data

Smith, Daniel P., 1980–
   On the job : behind the stars of the Chicago Police Department /
by Daniel P. Smith. — 1st ed.

   p. : ill. ; cm.

   Includes index.
   ISBN-13: 978-1-893121-12-6
   ISBN-10: 1-893121-12-7

1. Chicago (Ill.). Police Dept—History. 2. Police—Illinois—Chicago—Biography. 3. Law enforcement—Illinois—Chicago. I. Title.

HV8148.C4 S65 2007

363.2/09773/11   2007923443

11 10 09 08   10 9 8 7 6 5 4 3 2 1

For my big brother

PART 3

WHO ARE WE? ORGANIZATION AND CULTURE OF THE CHICAGO POLICE DEPARTMENT

PART 4

POLICE WORK, THE PERSON, THE LIFE, AND THE SPIRIT

Twelve Steps to a Better Cop: Detective Jim Rohrlack
He told the man to drop the knife, and when he didn't, Jim Rohrlack fired. In subsequent years, a turbulent tailspin sent Rohrlack to the bottle, twelve steps, and a second chance at life. In then end, Rohrlack claims, he emerged a better cop.

A Black and White Issue: Sergeant Joe Barnes Jr.
Joe Barnes Jr. calls it as he sees it—a ball's a ball and a strike's a strike. And the world, he says, claims a universal strike zone, one that transcends creed, class, and race and drives him to take the negative off Chicago's streets.

Faith: Detective Mike Cummins
Once a high school religion teacher, Mike Cummins left the world of academia and religious tenets to join the Chicago Police. His eyes now opened after a dozen years on the job, Mike Cummins cannot look away.

Meaningful Work: Father Tom Nangle, CPD Chaplain
Father Tom Nangle reports he has an officer pull him aside almost daily to tell him, "You might not believe it, Father, but I pray every day." But Nangle, the CPD's Chaplain for over two decades, sees no reason to question the spirit and soul of Chicago's officers.

➤ *Brothers Joe and Bill Mahoney, circa 1960.*
Courtesy of the Mahoney family

➤ *Three generations of Chicago Police Officers (Left to Right): Tommy McIntyre, Bobby Smith, Bill Mahoney, and John McIntyre.*
Courtesy of the Mahoney family

ROLL CALL

We cannot select the families we are born into—the traditions that pervade the family dynamic, the unwritten codes that govern our loyalties. I was born into an Irish-Catholic family in Chicago. God reigned supreme. The Cubs, Bears, and Notre Dame football were to be admired. Your cousins were to be as near to you as brothers and sisters. Grandma was queen. And the family business was the Chicago Police Department.

Two of my three great uncles were. Two of my three uncles are. My estranged father was. My only brother is. A Chicago cop. Despite a bloodline that urged me to become a Chicago cop, I could not bring myself to carry on the family tradition. Though lacking the assertive nature necessary to become a cop in one of the world's most dangerous cities and the mental makeup to challenge a city notorious for its criminal action, I maintain a close relationship and fascination with the Chicago Police Department, its members, and the proud tradition the force carries to this day. At the least, my heredity assures me of that.

My great uncle Bill Mahoney retired as one of the city's five deputy superintendents, while his older brother Joe was a respected detective and later a lieutenant. My uncle John McIntyre was a lifetime patrol officer— first on Chicago's West Side, one of the city's most infamous crime dens, and then in the area near venerable Wrigley Field—while another uncle, Tommy McIntyre, has spent the most recent years of his career as a cold-case detective on numerous highly publicized investigations. Often, in an ironic twist, Tommy found himself studying unsolved crimes with Uncle Joe's handwritten notes covering the file—one generation attempting to unpack the other's mysteries. My older brother, meanwhile, spent many years in a specialized city unit called Special Operations, a group devoted to hot spots in different areas of the city, before moving to Gang Intelligence, another citywide unit. I often say my brother was blessed with two natural gifts: an athletic ease that allowed him to be an 11-year-old switch hitter, and a slightly crooked mind (surviving a turbulent adolescence) that aided his efforts in police work. It's frequently true: the best cops today often dabbled in some misdeeds themselves as youths or knew the neighborhood's unwritten street codes well before entering law enforcement. They know how the system really works, inherently possessing a sense of criminal tendencies, and when they don the Chicago Police Department star, they call upon an intuition to address crime.

While others in the Mahoney family lineage took different routes— union jobs in professional fields such as education—the family business remained strong as each generation fielded its own participants into the department—a brother here, a cousin there, and then some of our sisters married cops. We are proud to say we were a Chicago Police family. That means something in this city, affording instant credibility and, right or not, a degree of respect. Growing up on the city's Northwest Side, I could say my uncles were Chicago cops and my brother was, too; in an unexplainable way, those with whom I was communicating would stand a little taller, and so would I. Since they were coppers, I, indirectly, was as well. True, the badges my family members wore said Chicago. But more than that, they represented a Mahoney family legacy—to protect the city that housed our families and our futures. This wasn't *their* city. It was *our* city. Most cop families like ours hold the same sentiment, whether they're from Edison Park, Morgan Park, Logan Square, or Garfield Ridge. There's a strong pride in being a Chicago Police family and an even stronger pride in all that the city represents.

On a June night in 2001, I became a Chicago policeman for a night. Sporting a bulletproof vest and with a Maglite in my hand ("Here," my brother directed, "if you need to defend yourself, use this."), I shadowed my brother and his partner, Dave Kumiega, from 6 P.M. to 2 A.M. At the time, my brother served on the 25th District's Tact Team, a plainclothes unit in one of the city's most active districts, an expansive neighborhood with an extremely diverse population—blacks, Hispanics, whites, and various immigrants. (The 25th District's north boundary was also a mere two blocks from the home where my brother and I grew up with our sister, mother, and grandmother.) Fifteen minutes out of the station, we had our first call—a homicide. A 17-year-old had shot his stepfather in the mouth, execution style.

My brother, never one to shelter me from gore and always curious about crime (another of his intrinsic traits), asked the sergeant at the site of the murder if I could see the body in the basement. Seeing my first dead body outside of a funeral home, I briefly studied the middle-aged Hispanic man, half his pale frame hanging off the bed and his white cotton tee covered in dull red blood. To my dismay, I had little reaction, viewing this man's body as something different from my living existence; in fact, I thought he best resembled a wax museum figure rather than a recently active human.

As I looked to my left, I saw officers moving about—one collecting evidence along the bar, another speaking to a teenage girl. Then, I saw a woman, her white jogging pants covered in blood to match her stained hands, and I caught a clear look at her face. Her eyes focused ahead, her mouth pushing out words to a detective. Then, I knew. She was the wife. She was the mother. This was a very real event. And this is what my brother and others like him see regularly. Each day, Chicago officers step out of their homes, temporarily leaving one life behind for another more dangerous one, unaware of what lies ahead.

Far from perfect, Chicago Police officers have battled their public troubles, from corruption to brutality, both present and past. Private lives, meanwhile, are too often laced with alcoholism and divorce (both of which pervaded my early life as a cop's son), and the emotional whiplash of struggling with crime every day takes a toll on the psyche. As with any profession—law, clergy, and medicine, for instance—all members do not necessarily maintain a "by the book" standard of excellence. Some cheat. Some steal. Some are lazy. Some simply don't comprehend the full scope of the work. The Chicago Police Department is not immune to such indignity. The crooked cop exists, and when he is caught, the media generally lead the stone throwing for others to follow suit. Yet, just as a blanket statement praising all officers as heroes is inaccurate, so too is a blanket statement labeling all as donut-eating, prejudiced crooks. The vast majority of Chicago officers, as I hope this book shows, are well-intentioned, sincere, talented, and proud individuals. More often than not, officers stand committed to enforcing the laws as best they can with all the resources available. In an active urban center such as Chicago, it would be naive to suggest that Chicago's officers do it by the book each day, but then strong police work rarely follows a clean and orderly path—there's a casual chat with this criminal, an interrogation of that one; the emotional toll of an unsolved crime, the prevention of ones to come; and public and media often skeptical of officers' moves and best intentions. Police work remains as blue-collar a job as there is, despite all the suits and ties one sees on television.

My purpose in writing this book is to share with you, the reader, stories of how Chicago's police officers balance all that the job demands— emotionally, physically, spiritually, and psychologically. Some bad. Some good. Some ugly. All real. Yet, this is not an attempt to discuss "the day in a life of a Chicago cop." Nor is this an exposition on what cops do and why they do it. Rather, *On the Job* attempts to show you the interworkings of one of history's most storied professions in one of the world's most storied cities and to do so in the most truthful of lights. Put that together, and you have a book about what Chicago Police officers bring to the job and take from the job, and how their work and personal lives coexist. Finally, in writing *On the Job*, I seek to do my lineage proud.

THE CHICAGO WAY:
POLICE WORK IN THE
URBAN LANDSCAPE

──────────────★──────────────

*Chicago, ever since prohibition, has had this remarkable
history of no line between what is legal and illegal.*
　　　　　　　　　—Studs Terkel in *Battleground Chicago*

*For heaven's sake, catch me before I kill more, I cannot
control myself.*
　　　　　　　　　—Scribbled in lipstick by murderer
　　　　　　　　　William Heirens on the wall of a victim's home

*The policeman isn't there to create disorder; the policeman
is there to preserve disorder.*
　　　　　　　　　—Late Chicago Mayor Richard J. Daley

──────────────★──────────────

For better or worse, we are Capone's city as much as Daley's or Jordan's. A
history of criminal figures and events engraved in its existence, Chicago is
identified for its murders over its mayors, its schemes over its superstars. Latin
Kings. Disciples. El Rukn. Heroin. Gacy. Speck. The Outfit. St. Valentine's Day.

The city's criminal history has reached fabled proportions, a product
of Hollywood as much as Chicago's own acceptance—and sometimes
celebration—of its dim underbelly. Outsiders, having been asked about their
knowledge of Chicago, have been known to form a gun with their fingers and
say "bang."

"That's Chicago," as Billy Flynn would say.

"It's easy to add to the myth because Chicago is a town defined by its history of being tough. It's not San Francisco or Los Angeles—it's a real 'American' city. New York, even, is more cosmopolitan and international," says author Frank Kusch, an observer of Chicago from his vantage point over the Canadian border.

Adds Chicago author Richard Lindberg: "There is a Chicago way—even among the most articulate—an alertness to the whole issue of violence and brutality that dots our city. This is still a meat-and-potatoes town and Chicago's a product of its industrial background—the old memories and impressions are genetic in the culture."

Criminal Chicago

Chicago's criminal history roots itself in the city's frontier spirit from the mid-1800s. While the city has never been mistaken for Wyatt Earp's Wild West, it has nevertheless entertained a coarse image throughout its history. In the mid-nineteenth century, the city's newspapers were filled with reports of thefts, rapes, murders, and arson, each tale underlining the fact that Chicago's criminal streak flourished. In 1840, the city held its first public hanging, with 2500 in attendance—over half of the city's reported 4400 citizens—confirming Chicago's recognition of crime as well as its firm stomach for handling the darker side of life. Vice, meanwhile, was not contained to backrooms; rather, gambling, prostitution, and other assorted criminal ventures prospered in plain view.[1]

As the decades of the nineteenth century moved ahead, lawlessness further entrenched itself in the city's lore. The Haymarket Affair in 1886, a movement attempting to secure workers an eight-hour day, pit Chicago's undermanned police force against a horde of unionists, reformers, and socialists. When the two sides clashed, a bomb hurled at police touched off a succession of chaos. Sixty officers were injured and eight killed, joining an undetermined number of protestors killed or wounded.[2] In the 1890s, the Levee District between 18th and 22nd Streets earned repute as Chicago's most brazen display of vice, bringing worldwide visitors and attention to the city's criminal activity. Chicagoans and the city hierarchy professed an acceptance of vice, so long as it remained in pockets of the city.

"The disreputable women, the pickpockets and petty thieves are better 'bunched' in one section of the city than scattered all over it," said the *Chicago Chronicle* in 1899. "The police know where to find them. Respectable people know how to avoid them."[3]

As such, misdeeds thrived in some districts under the open eyes of the city and its visitors. With its containment approach and rather blasé attitude, Chicago's criminality only further engrained itself into the city's psyche and history, as well as dictating police response.

"A man born in the city slums [with] only a grade school education probably did not share the same moralistic views about wagering as a clergyman or Gold Coast reformer," writes Richard Lindberg in *To Serve and Collect*. "The perception of the seriousness of the crime was frequently a determinant in the police response."[4]

As early as the 1880s, a burgeoning gang scene developed in such historic neighborhoods as Bridgeport and Back of the Yards on the South Side, where ruffians raided street peddlers and robbed men leaving work at the stockyards. By the 1920s, an estimated 1300 gangs existed in Chicago, the vast majority considered social clubs such as the Hamburg Club and the Old Rose Athletic Club.[5] The Ragen's Colts, a group spurring from the Morgan Athletic Club and at the center of the city's 1919 race riot, claimed many members that would later become skilled politicians and labor representatives, wiggling their way into Chicago's political landscape, creating a patronage army, and demonstrating the city hierarchy's ever-increasing dealings with illicit factions. Such gangs served the foundation for Chicago's most infamous criminal unit,

➤ *Eerie crime is nothing new to members of the Chicago Police Department. A threatening note etched on the wall of a city home reads, "I will kill you," while a knife holds a picture of the intended target.*
Courtesy of Art Hannus

The Outfit, and transferred Chicago's reputation as a place of lawlessness into a city of underworld authority.

Indeed, it is Alphonse Capone who stands among the city's most dominant figures—criminal or otherwise. The Brooklyn-born Capone arrived in Chicago in 1919, settling with his Irish wife and infant son at 7244 S. Prairie Avenue. Capone's decade-long reign in Chicago was characterized by dominance in city matters as well as criminal inventiveness and ruthlessness. From 1925 to 1930, Capone took charge of the fleeing John Torrio's empire, which included speakeasies, gambling dens, brothels, and breweries, accumulating an estimated annual income of nearly $100 million. Yet, Capone also earned public trust for his Depression-era soup kitchens and widespread generosity, lending credence to Chicago scribe Nelson Algren's words: "For always [Chicago's] villains have hearts of gold and all our heroes are slightly tainted."[6]

On Valentine's Day 1929, Capone's men entered rival gang leader "Bugs" Moran's garage and committed an act forever etched in city lore. Disguised as Chicago Police officers, the four Capone underlings ordered the seven inhabitants to face the wall and fired over 150 bullets into their victims.

The murder, sensationalized by such newspaper headlines as "MASSACRE," solidified the city's penchant for violence as well as Capone's image as a vicious gangland leader, even prompting *Chicago Tribune* reporter Ridgely Hunt to claim that Capone "raised murder to the level of a national spectator sport."[7]

The St. Valentine's Day Massacre, which led to the police department's creation of a lab expressly to solve the crime, also highlighted the Chicago Outfit's unique and lasting commitment to crime on display. Where the New York mob has often preferred to hide victims' bodies, the Chicago Outfit has appeared forever proud of its work, allowing such carnage to remain untouched and the message to arrive without debate.

With Capone, Chicago inherited a criminal legacy that survives to this day, one defined by gunshots and gore. The mythical stature of Chicago's criminal landscape sheds light on the city's nostalgic yearning to be seen as tough, rugged, and hardnosed. A firm handshake town. A don't-back-down town. A city where fistfights and tenacity define one's passage. As much as many Chicagoans may seek a more cosmopolitan image, the city has long refused to abandon its gritty character—a fact evident in mayors ruling like dictators, baton-wielding police, and territorial defense of neighborhood codes.

That's Chicago.

"Once you've come to be a part of this particular parch," Algren sang of

➤ *Chicago Police officers stand ready with their horses (circa 1910).*
Courtesy of the Chicago Public Library, Special Collections and Preservation Division

Chicago, "you'll never love another. Like loving a woman with a broken nose, you may well find lovelier lovelies. But never a lovely so real."[8]

Subsequent decades have done little to shed the city's jagged, tumbling, robust aura. There are the oft-reported cases of Richard Speck, who in the summer of 1966 methodically murdered eight Chicago nursing students, as well as John Wayne Gacy, the mass-murdering businessman who buried the remains of his 30 victims under the crawlspace of his Northwest Side home. Such incidents have only advanced Chicago's criminal identification, labeling it as the city that works outside the law.

"When [former Chicago Mayor] Big Bill Thompson put in the fix for Capone he tied the town to the rackets for keeps," said Algren of the wonderfully corrupt Thompson

"The best any mayor can do with the city since is just to keep it in repair . . . And since it's a ninth-inning town, the ball game never being over till the last man is out, it remains Jane Addams' town as well as Big Bill's. The ball game isn't over yet. But it's a rigged ball game."[9]

Chicago—As *They* Know It

While some cases secure national and global headlines, the daily grind of Chicago's criminal element serves just as much vice and disregard. As drugs pressed their way into the social element during the 1970s and 1980s, Chicago's street gangs, once formed as protective clubs and unified fronts against civil strife, became mini-corporations. Money commanded the gang's attention and the battle for lucrative drug territory and connections allowed such Chicago-based gangs as the Latin Kings and Vice Lords to spread drugs and violence throughout Chicago neighborhoods, contributing to a high of 747 homicides in 1986.[10] Today, the Chicago Police Department reports (perhaps modestly) that an estimated 38,000 members comprise the city's 40 active street gangs, an important power source in many neighborhoods and social units that have become so savvy that the city's recent real estate boom has served an opportune moment to launder drug money through home sales while the Internet has provided a successful recruitment and internal communications tool.

Though street gangs represent a portion of Chicago's violent activities, crime in the city often claims neither colors nor relationships—it spreads among the citizenry with thefts, assaults, drug offenses, and domestic quarrels. In 2004, Chicago received nearly 5.3 million calls for emergency service, an average of nearly two calls for every resident.[11] Uniformed officers answer two-thirds of those calls, far more than their counterparts in other cities. While many Chicagoans enjoyed a lovely summer night on Saturday, June 3, 2006, Chicago Police officers in the West Side's 11th District had few moments of respite on the 4 P.M.–midnight shift: *(See chart on page 11.)*

On the Job in Chicago

Indeed, just as much a part of Chicago's mythic criminal culture stands a police department charged with a reputation of its own—tough, gritty, and

➤ *Residents fill the West Side's Fillmore Police Station in 1948 to reclaim stolen goods.*
Courtesy of the Chicago Public Library, Special Collections and Preservation Division

My Alarm
4:04:
Selling Narcotics
4:06:
Criminal
Damage to
Property
4:08:
Domestic
Disturbance
4:09:
Citizen Holding
Offender
4:12: Disturbance
4:15:
Selling Narcotics
4:15: Theft
Report
4:17: Disturbance
4:18: Disturbance
4:20: Theft
Report
4:22:
Burglary in
Progress
4:27:
Selling Narcotics
4:31:
Domestic
Disturbance
4:31:
Selling Narcotics
4:33:
Selling Narcotics
4:35: Assault
4:35: Burglary in
Progress
4:38: Domestic
Disturbance
4:39: Assault
4:41:
Battery in
Progress
4:45: Selling
Narcotics
4:49:
Selling Narcotics
4:53:
Assault in
Progress
4:53: Selling
Narcotics
4:59:
Burglary Alarm
5:06:
Burglary in
Progress
5:12: Disturbance
5:15:
Auto Accident
5:22
Theft in Progress
5:24:
Selling Narcotics
5:34:
Vice Complaints
in Progress

5:40:
Criminal
Damage to
Property
5:40:
Assault in
Progress
5:42:
Domestic
Disturbance
5:42:
Auto Accident
5:49:
Domestic
Battery
5:50:
Auto Accident
5:50: Disturbance
5:57:
Domestic
Disturbance
6:02: Gambling
6:04: Theft
Report
6:09:
Auto Accident
6:13: Fire
6:13:
Selling Narcotics
6:18:
Domestic
Disturbance
6:18:
Domestic
Battery
6:19:
Selling Narcotics
6:19:
Disturbance
6:26:
Child Left Alone
6:27: Selling
Narcotics
6:31: Gambling
6:37:
Selling Narcotics
6:40:
Selling Narcotics
6:53: Disturbance
6:53:
Auto Accident
6:54: Shots Fired
7:03: Disturbance
7:08:
Burglary Alarm
7:16:
Auto Accident
7:20: Shots Fired
7:25: Disturbance
7:26:
Selling Narcotics
7:30: Assault
7:30:
Burglary Alarm
7:30: Disturbance
7:36:
Selling Narcotics

7:38: Assault
7:41:
Selling Narcotics
7:42:
Selling Narcotics
7:44:
Vice in Progress
7:44:
Well Being
Check
7:45: Disturbance
7:46:
Holding
Offender
7:46: Disturbance
7:47: Assault
Assault in
Progress
7:52:
Battery in
Progress
7:53:
Assault in
Progress
7:53: Battery
7:58: Disturbance
8:00:
Battery in
Progress
8:02: Disturbance
8:05:
Burglary Alarm
8:09: Disturbance
8:10:
Holding
Offender
8:11:
Selling Narcotics
8:12: Disturbance
8:13:
Vice in Progress
8:16: Disturbance
8:17: Disturbance
8:19: Battery
8:20:
Selling Narcotics
8:21: Assault
8:22:
Reckless Driving
8:24:
Battery in
Progress
8:29: Battery in
Progress
8:35:
Person with
Knife
8:37:
Person Calling
for Help
8:37:
Selling Narcotics
8:39:
Domestic
Disturbance
8:39: Domestic
Battery

8:42: Disturbance
8:45: Disturbance
8:47:
Domestic
Battery
8:50: Gambling
8:53:
Selling Narcotics
8:57:
Gang/Narcotics
Loitering
8:58:
Gang/Narcotics
Loitering
8:59:
Vice in Progress
8:59:
Theft in Progress
9:00: Gambling
9:00:
Selling Narcotics
9:02: Selling
Narcotics
9:03: Disturbance
9:03: Assault
9:12: Theft
Report
9:12: Disturbance
9:17: Disturbance
9:20: Fire
9:22:
Auto Accident
9:23:
Auto Accident
9:28:
Auto Accident
9:35: Assault
9:37: Disturbance
9:38:
Selling Narcotics
9:48:
Animal Abuse
9:48:
Selling Narcotics
9:48:
Burglary Report
9:49: Assault
9:50:
Selling Narcotics
9:54:
Burglary Report
10:09:
Disturbance
10:15: Shots
Fired
10:16:
Disturbance
10:16:
Disturbance
10:17:
Battery in
Progress
10:21:
Criminal
Trespassing
10:21:
Disturbance

10:23:
Disturbance
10:25:
Prostitution
10:25:
Missing Person
10:25:
Disturbance
10:25:
Auto Accident
10:28:
Burglary Report
10:29:
Prostitution
10:30: DUI
10:30:
Prostitution
10:32: Lost
Person
10:32:
Assault in
Progress
10:36: Foot
Pursuit
10:36:
Assault in
Progress
10:36: DUI
10:37:
Domestic
Battery
10:37:
Disturbance
10:39:
Disturbance
10:41: Burglary
Report
10:44: Auto
Accident
10:44:
Disturbance
10:44: Fire
10:47: Gang
Disturbance
10:48: Battery
Report
10:51: Auto
Accident
10:53: Domestic
Battery
10:56:
Disturbance
10:57:
Disturbance
10:57: Burglary
Report
10:57:
Disturbance
10:59: Assault
11:01:
Disturbance
11:02:
Assist Citizen
11:03:
Selling Narcotics
11:04:
Gang/Narcotics

Loitering
11:07:
Disturbance
11:09:
Disturbance
11:11:
Battery Report
11:11:
Selling Narcotics
11:12:
Disturbance
11:13:
Disturbance
11:14: Drag
Racing
11:18:
Disturbance
11:18:
Disturbance
11:19:
Disturbance
11:19:
Disturbance
11:21:
Gang/Narcotics
Loitering
11:21:
Disturbance
11:23:
Disturbance
11:24:
Domestic
Disturbance
11:24: Drag
Racing
11:26:
Auto Accident
11:27:
Selling Narcotics
11:30:
Selling Narcotics
11:30: Robbery
11:33:
Disturbance
11:35: Battery
11:36:
Disturbance
11:37:
Domestic
Disturbance
11:40:
Disturbance
11:41:
Selling Narcotics
11:44:
Disturbance
11:49:
Shot Fired
(followed by
Foot Pursuit)
11:50: Gambling
11:52:
Disturbance
11:59: Sex
Offense

diligent among the many characteristics that just as easily define the city itself. Dealing with one of the nation's most active criminal landscapes, where guns, drugs, and gangs infect every block of the city's 3,400 miles of streets, the life of a Chicago officer leads to daily encounters with crime and disruption; in the process, Chicago officers have emerged with a legend all their own.

"Chicago officers are a bit bigger than life," says author Frank Kusch. "Toughness and hard work defines Chicago and its people. And the city's cops cannot be separated from that. Ask any of the CPD and they're from the streets, the alleys, the curbs."

Chicago is a city where legends are born of those donning a CPD star. Former Superintendent LeRoy Martin once called the Chicago Police "the toughest gang in town." Consider Captain Frank Pape, perhaps the city's most famous officer, who claimed involvement in 15 gunfights, killing nine criminals in the process. Or Joe DiLeonardi, the one-time homicide detective and acting superintendent, who rose up the ranks with a combination of intelligence and courage. Or Jack Muller, the self-titled "world's most famous cop," who took a bullet in the skull and lived to challenge City Hall and the status quo. Pape, DiLeonardi, and Muller represent the few committing their memories to print; far more officers lead just as storied, colorful lives yet remain tight-lipped on the career and the tales that accompany the journey.

Perhaps the defining event in the city's police department history remains the 1968 Democratic National Convention, a week that, for better or worse, labeled the city, police department, and individual officers with a reputation for no-nonsense—some would say brutish—tactics. "People often have a vague idea of what happened in 1968—it was bad and the police weren't good," says Kusch, whose *Battleground Chicago* documents police action during convention week.

While conflict between citizens and police had long been a part of the city and national landscape and Chicagoans frequently took on an unenthusiastic view of outsiders, the 1960s placed explosives under the battleground, the police playing the visible face of the detested "establishment." The much publicized charge into Chicago of the student-radical Yippies coincided with Mayor Richard J. Daley's demand that Chicago officers follow his directives and command the streets. (Perhaps Daley's biggest gaffe came with the order to remove the protestors from Lincoln Park, thereby sending a mob of youth throughout Chicago's streets and creating conflict rather than containment.) More often than not, Chicago's officers have been viewed as violent, mechanical souls during convention week, a charge Kusch discovered to be overwhelming faulty.

"I didn't get a sense that they had a choice," said Kusch. "Still, the police weren't these unthinking guys to be directed like stick figures. They had certain pressures on them from family, people in their neighborhoods, and that mitigated against the worst circumstances of 1968."

What's more, Chicago's officers during the 1968 convention were viewed to be excessive in their force. Illinois State Senator Adlai Stevenson III called the city's police "Chicago's shame," while others tagged the department "the

➢ *Captain Frank Pape (right, standing with former Chicago Police officer Art Hannus) is among the most legendary of Chicago Police officers. In his 39-year Chicago Police career, Pape, who held his dying partner in his arms after a 1945 shootout with an armed robber, sent over 300 men to prison and was involved in 16 shootouts, killing nine suspects. His Chicago Police career served as the basis for the "M Squad" television series. In 2000, Pape passed away at the age of 91.*
Courtesy of Art Hannus

storm troopers in blue."[12] Though baited by protestors, captured by the media, and placed under the uncompromising thumb of Mayor Daley, Chicago officers have also been heralded for their restraint. Despite all the bedlam of convention week, not one fatality occurred—a surprising contrast to the 1968 Republican Convention in Miami that witnessed four deaths. Despite facts and the objective admissions of some, the 1968 DNC has continued to mark the Chicago Police

Department with an unmistakable reputation for tough love with its people and a baton-to-the-gut for its invaders.

"Convention week made the Chicago Police Department bigger than life, even though it may have soiled some of the mystique," said Kusch. "As times change, people fear what's going on and the Chicago Police Department is somewhat emblematic of a group that doesn't overthink stuff. That's necessary, even though no one wants to talk about it."

As Chicago has evolved, so too has its police department. Today's officer must not only possess the mind and body to handle the daily rigors of police work, but also the gifts of patience, law acumen, and community relations. "Where spit and polish may go a long way in some districts, in others it's about blood and guts," said former Chicago officer Gina Gallo.[13]

The flight of working-class families to the suburbs throughout the 1950s, '60s, and '70s left Chicago struggling with its identity. The city of neighborhoods and ethnic enclaves was losing its grip; neighborhoods—such as Englewood on the south, Austin to the west, and Rogers Park up north—witnessed changing populations, shifting community needs, and new social issues, which forced officers into redefined roles. The gentrification of recent years in Chicago has once again transitioned community compositions and police responsibilities—Humboldt Park, Pilsen, Garfield Park, and Bridgeport are among the many historic Chicago neighborhoods undergoing demographic shifts and demanding that officers meet new community needs. Such transitions follow similar changes in other neighborhoods, including Wicker Park, the South Loop, Lincoln Park, and Taylor Street. These areas, once filled with immigrants and families, are witnessing an influx of fresh faces that crowd streets with SUVs and boutiques that sit below loft-style condos. Slowly, in Chicago, a town where the tavern and church once held equal dominance, the altars sit unused and the corner pubs have given way to clubs and wine bars. In the process, Chicago police officers have been forced to mature as well.

The Chicago Way

On the night of Richard J. Daley's mayoral victory in 1955, 43rd Ward Democratic boss Paddy Bauler reminded the city's people from his barstool, "Chicago ain't ready for reform." As much as the city has developed recent touches of brilliance and culture—Millennium Park, high-rise Loop condos, and spin classes on the lakefront over softball games in the park (please leave the glove at home)—the city remains

➤ *Chicago Police officers of the Jefferson Township Hall's 36th Precinct pose for a photo (circa 1900). Early Chicago Police officers were encouraged to handle their patrol beats physically, a stark contrast to today's hands-off policies.*
Courtesy of the Chicago Public Library, Special Collections and Preservation Division

close to its roots as a hustler's town, a fighter's town. Chicago continues to grapple with a legacy that contains as much hypocrisy, Outfit ties, political corruption, and vice as it does affability, work ethic, civic spirit, and virtue. The city still condemns the criminal acts while simultaneously savoring the perception it brings—one doesn't mess with Chicago. We live here with blue-collar hands, resilient spirits, and rugged souls touting our toughness as well as our international flair. We want it both ways: a first-class city with first-class prizefighters.

And while the city's police department, an equal symbol of our city's desires and realities, has endured fire, both on the streets and in public opinion polls, it has nevertheless secured a degree of public appreciation and understanding that often passes unsaid. "For the masses who do the city's labor also keep the city's heart," Algren wrote.[14] Many Chicagoans criticize their police department for force, brevity, or approach, yet they support, honor, and value the group's efforts. Again, the split—we want tough officers; we just don't want them to be tough on us.

"People respect toughness, especially in Chicago," said Kusch. "They respect

➤ *Around Chicago, gentrification has placed high-priced homes alongside dilapidated buildings and vacant, weed-infested lots. In Chicago's historic Italian neighborhood based on Taylor Street, the ABLA public housing units await destruction in the shadow the Sears Tower, while red brick townhouses bloom from the vacant lots. The gentrification of such neighborhoods has demanded that Chicago officers fill new roles in the face of shifting demographics and community needs.*

Courtesy of Daniel P. Smith

people who take a stand, no matter what side. Just as in 1968, people respected what the police did and they understood. Generally, I found people to have a good feeling about the Chicago Police Department. Fear, yes, but it's in context."

And so Chicago's police officers charge along, inhabiting a changing world, nation, and city. They do so guarding a metropolis clamoring with three million people, every possible concoction of the human mind making an appearance at some time, in some place. Like Brian Spreng, officers encounter a reality where bullets fly and questions follow; like Dave Kumiega, they seek entry into the underworld of Chicago's gang culture; like Miguel Rios, they defend their own, face life-altering situations, and sometimes tragic results; like C.K. Rojas, a former officer in rural North Carolina, they enter the city with passion and spirit, their life's goals tucked next to the soul and the star; and like Art Hannus, officers seek to balance career demands with life ambitions.

Chicago is still on the make and it cannot divorce itself from its past. Its toughness, its grit, its criminal culture survive, and its police department persists in the face of it all.

After all, that's Chicago.

IMAGINATION MEETS REALITY: OFFICER BRIAN SPRENG

———————————————★———————————————

Brian Spreng recalls his early days on the job with a sigh. "I thought it would be more hands-on. I thought it'd be non-stop," he says shaking his head. "And it just wasn't; it was boring."

Spreng arrived in the Northwest Side's 25th District just after Thanksgiving with the frigid air of Chicago casting its shadow, a sign that weather would play its part in slowing crime. In his first two weeks, Spreng had only one arrest—a misdemeanor for a domestic dispute. He underwent the typical rookie schedule—working different beats each day, gathering a sense of the expansive district, and exploring the rights and wrongs of police work outside of the academy's classrooms.

Quickly, Spreng noticed that his police life would not only stand in contrast to the cop shows on television, but that his days and nights may not even be as active as the ones others in his graduating academy class were experiencing in other districts. While his fellow rookies were getting a gun here, a drug bust there—and talking about it—Spreng could offer little to the discussion. Learning the north-south streets that start with K, L, M, and N. Gaining an understanding of one gang's particulars over another. Touching up on protocol, writing reports, but no real action, he admits.

"Yeah, I kept on wondering what I was doing wrong. I kept wondering when things would pick up, when I'd get that real police action," says Spreng.

But as most veteran coppers tell, the silence often means a storm lurks behind. When things are calm, that's when the action will jump out and grab hold of life.

———————————————★———————————————

Brian Spreng covers his boyish grin and stark blond hair with a Chicago Cubs baseball cap as he sips an Oreo milk shake. He laughs often and flashes a bashful grin. He's a warm presence, a kind man who offers "pleases" and "thank yous" to the waitress and reminisces about coming to Petersen's, an antique Oak Park ice cream parlor, since his boyhood days.

"But I grew up south of the tracks," he says, noting his more modest upbringing in neighboring River Forest, the near western suburb overflowing with wide lawns and classical homes. "Most of my extended family's in Philly though. My grandpa and uncle were firemen there, but as far as I know, I'm the first cop in the family—Chicago or elsewhere." Despite his husky build, Spreng remains as unassuming as the next guy. A simple face in a moving crowd.

"When we got out of the [Chicago Police] academy," he says, "the other guys would talk about the guns they'd gotten or the drug bust they'd had and I didn't have much to say. I hadn't done much of anything in those early days. Then, I'd ask myself, 'What am I doing wrong? How come they're so good and I suck?'"

In fact, those early days and weeks of a rookie Chicago officer contain the necessary clash of reality and imagination, a reconciliation of what the job is and what the young cop envisioned it would be. Early on, police realize that every day doesn't yield a major drug bust or gun arrest. Every shift endures its own life, its own mix of excitement, boredom, and indifference. The Clint Eastwood stuff of movies remains locked in both Hollywood and the mind's far-reaching fantasy.

"I always wanted to be a Chicago cop," says Spreng, a 30-year-old with two years on the job. "I knew that Chicago was where real police work was, and ever since I was young I wanted to be a part of that."

After taking the Chicago Police test in 2001, Spreng began his training at the city's police academy in April 2003. A four-year veteran of the United States Marine Corps, he joined the Chicago Police Department for the same reasons he joined the military.

"I just kind of always had this desire to serve, whether it be for country or community," Spreng says, acknowledging the embarrassment in relaying such an innocent statement. "The Marines are the best of the best, and that's why I always wanted to be a Chicago cop, too."

And yet, Spreng spent his early days in the 25th District both disillusioned and disappointed, facing thoughts of what would be and what really existed on Chicago's streets.

"I thought I'd be getting guns and drugs every day, but it's not as easy as you'd think."

➢ *A class of CPD cadets poses in the Navy Pier ballroom following their academy graduation ceremony. The following day, the newly minted patrol officers report to districts around the city to begin their Chicago Police careers. For Brian Spreng that meant the 25th District.*

Courtesy of the Smith Family

Fate, however, has an odd way of determining our path, of pushing us in one direction when others are before us. On the night of Sunday, December 14, 2003, fate led Brian Spreng into a moment of intensity, color, and peril.

"It was one of those first real cold nights of winter," recalls Spreng of his 16th day on the job. In remembering a day that has defined his early police career, if not his life, Spreng speaks clearly and succinctly. He begins to share his story in chronological fashion, without any pause to reconsider the day's order.

"We were driving south toward Division and we heard seven or eight gunshots. I just looked at my FTO [Field Training Officer]. I knew from the military that those were gunshots; they weren't fireworks."

Turning onto Division Street, the pair began heading east, soon spotting two guys running—backs turned—in the direction of their squad car. Both men continued firing into a corner restaurant. Spreng and his partner pulled the car into the mouth of an alley between Pulaski Road and Keystone Avenue. The men continued to shoot and run, unaware of their movement into a police squad car.

"My heart was pounding and we started yelling 'Drop the guns.' They didn't hear us, but we kept yelling anyway," says Spreng. "Then, one guy heard us, turned around, and fired. His buddy ducked behind a car. But we fired our weapons at the guy still out in the open, the same guy who had first fired at us. He started falling down and then the other guy got up and started walking out from behind the car and headed down the alley. Out of the corner of my eye, I could see him hiding in the second yard."

In moments, other officers arrived on the scene and Spreng directed his focus to the man now hiding in a backyard. Officers began yelling at the suspect to get down on the ground, but he took off, running south on Keystone Avenue. Spreng gave chase.

"I don't know if I was sprinting or jogging or if he was either," says Spreng. "I don't even remember thinking—just reacting, just relying on my instincts to guide me."

Police cars heading north on Keystone had the suspect pegged between Spreng's foot chase with two other district officers and their own cars. Cornered, the suspect stopped and began walking toward Spreng.

"I could see he didn't have the gun in his hands anymore, but he wouldn't listen to us and get down on the ground. We kept shouting at him and he ignored it."

Within seconds, a female officer rushed toward the suspect and tackled him from behind. The one man restrained, Spreng returned to the start of the scene to see cops surrounding a car, demanding that the second man relinquish his gun and get out from under the car. He eventually complied, and police seized both guns used in the shooting.

"Everything was in slow motion up to the point in which the guy shot at us. Then, it seemed like it was all moving at 100 miles per hour," says Spreng.

"They talk to you in the academy about having blinders on—you know, tunnel vision? I didn't hear my radio or anything. I was just so focused on that pursuit. I remember remarking earlier to my FTO how slow things seemed that day and then—boom—it happens. Absolute chaos."

Spreng shakes his head with eyes pointed downward. He remains amazed at how quickly an officer's life transfers from one extreme to another. Once the shock of the situation subsided, he began to realize the magnitude of the event. Sixteen days into the job, he had just been involved in a full-fledged shootout.

"For the first 30 minutes after, I was scared," he says. "I think that's the simple term to use for the immediate emotions I felt. My first thought was, I'm a probationary officer; I'm not supposed to fire my gun. I'm going to get fired."

He then began to replay the steps in his head. The approach to the scene. The spotting of the suspects firing their guns—first at the restaurant, then at him. The foot chase. His immediate playback gave way to a short-lived round of second-guessing.

"Eventually, I just said, 'No. We did everything right. We did our job and defended ourselves.'"

Spreng takes a deep breath. He stares down at his empty sandwich plate and then reaches for his Oreo milk shake.

"I was everything rolled into one that night," he says. "I was scared, excited, nervous—going through just every emotion you could imagine. You can never anticipate how something like this could go down and how you're going to feel when it's all done."

He takes a long sip, repeating something he's done numerous times at Petersen's Ice Cream Parlor since his childhood. He discusses finding the proper perspective for his actions, in full recognition that he did precisely what he was supposed to do.

"I got home at 10:30 the next morning and my adrenaline was still going. I called the people I care about—my family, some close friends—and told them what happened—not to brag but to just let them know what had happened," he says. "I didn't go to sleep for a few hours, either. I still had this adrenaline running through me. All of those gunshots kept me up for a while."

Now, over a year later, Brian Spreng continues dealing with the aftermath. The event could have had different results; fate might have determined a different resolution.

"Every day when I go to work now, I'm definitely making sure I'm going home in one piece," says Spreng. "It's not that I wasn't safe before or that I didn't value my safety, but now I'm more aware of that priority. I hold my personal safety and that of the other officers and my family much more sacred. Everything could've turned out much differently.

"I don't feel like Dirty Harry or anything. And I don't feel any different as a person. I did the right thing. But I do feel like I grew up a lot. Now that I've been through this and done what was necessary, I feel like I can handle just about anything on this job."

Spreng pauses and drops the napkin he's knotted up over the last minutes, the one he twisted around every finger on his left hand while relaying his story. He again takes hold of his Oreo shake and pulls it toward him for some final sips—perhaps finding comfort in the familiar. His youthful face doesn't match the story he's just told. He takes off his baseball cap to reveal a wealth of blond hair; he then runs his right hand over his head from front to back, scattering the hair in different directions.

"Being involved in a shooting," he begins, "is one of the most difficult things I could ever imagine doing—and it came only 16 days onto the job. I didn't take this job to fire my weapon, but that's what that day demanded."

Spreng has told his story over and over—to fellow officers, to cadets at the academy, to family and friends. Each time Spreng shares his story, the details arrive fluid and unchanged—street names, the time of day, the frigid air that touched his skin, the emotions that consumed him. He remembers it all. And still, each retelling brings with it a questioning, a doubt, a concern over the precision of his actions. Today is no different. The questioning begins as the night's action travels from his mind to his voice. He shares his doubts, but safely reaches his conclusion.

"But I did the right thing," he assures himself. "I did the right thing."

His Oreo shake finished, Spreng puts on a thick flannel coat, stands, and steadies the Cubs hat on his head. He steps toward the door, unaware of what fate has planned for him this evening.

FRONTLINES:
OFFICER DAVE KUMIEGA

──────────────────★──────────────────

It's late November 2004, and the 25th District is "up for grabs" (police talk denoting a battle for drug territory). Dave Kumiega, a member of the district's gang team, stands in the middle of it all—a vicious clash between different factions of the Vice Lords, one of Chicago's oldest gangs, the 4-Corner Hustlers, and the numerous other gangs that blanket the district's streets. "Shots fired" calls are up, armed robberies are up, and the struggle for lucrative drug corners takes its toll on police and gang members alike, putting everyone on edge.

Kumiega, a stocky 32-year-old who has spent his entire six-year career in the city's expansive 25th District, says this is about as bad as it gets. Continual criminal activity demanding a constant police presence coupled with decisive action.

Kumiega can't remember the last time he worked an eight-hour day, hasn't eaten a dinner with his family the same day he's worked in weeks, and surely can't recall his last full night of sleep. And yet, he can tell you the last time he got a burrito from a Mexican joint on Fullerton Avenue at 3 A.M. and ate it over paperwork at the station; these days, that's Kumiega's routine, more common than tucking his boys into bed. He's enduring the ripple effect of one crime's rock thrown into his life—one gun shot or drug trade affecting Kumiega, his wife, his kids—the ripples spreading outward as one sinking rock pushes, touches, and redirects the lives of so many.

And yet it's what Kumiega signed up for—the adrenaline of the hunt, the excitement, the good that could come of his actions.

"You want the good people in these neighborhoods to be taken care of," he says. "You want them to know you're doing all you can to clean things up, to make things better for them."

Perhaps, in time, creating a different ripple effect.

──────────────────★──────────────────

➢ *Graffiti art marks gang territory. Simply from the graffiti, many Chicago Police officers can define an area as a certain gang's stronghold as well as gain a pulse on gang relationships in the neighborhood.*
Courtesy of Daniel P. Smith

They come with names like Ty-fly, Tower, Sweet Pea, KK, Rank Animal, and Gordo. And Dave Kumiega seeks to know each one inside and out—their colors, their home, their girlfriend's home, their tattoos, their history, any piece of information that may help solve a crime or be used to gain critical information for an arrest.

Kumiega does it day and night alongside other Chicago Police officers attempting to infiltrate the secret world of the city, a complex weaving of nearly 40 street gangs throughout Chicago's vast cityscape. Kumiega plods through databases, seeking to connect the dots from one man and one crime to the next—laborious, tedious work that taxes the mind and demands a sharp memory, a keen eye, and, perhaps above all else, a commitment to the pursuit. This remains a passion for Kumiega, an officer on Chicago's frontlines who doesn't see things second- or third-hand or shy from the work that comes with his job as a member of the 25th District's gang team.

"I love that first-hand immediacy of police work," says Kumiega. "You're thinking ahead to discover what you can do to solve the problem, to make things right."

All of Kumiega's six-plus years with the Chicago Police Department have been spent on the streets of the 25th District, serving as the city's first line of defense against criminal activity. The district is a diverse neighborhood that contains all shades of humanity—with differences ranging from ethnicity and income to history and motivation. Its southeastern-most part includes West Humboldt Park, a predominantly Puerto Rican area, while the southwest corner of the district touches the city's predominantly African-American West Side. The northeastern section holds a melting pot of blue-collar immigrant families with backgrounds ranging from Mexican to Polish. The district's northwest corner consumes neighborhoods such as Montclare and Galewood where middle-class homes host tradespeople and city workers.

While one day for Kumiega may be spent researching the Latino gangs of West Humboldt Park, another will demand his best attempts to resolve a petty dispute between arguing Polish immigrants in the Belmont-Cragin neighborhood. The 25th District never lacks intriguing characters and plots. And Kumiega accepts his role in the drama.

"Some of the days it's constant excitement and adrenaline; other times, it's boring as hell," says Kumiega. "But it's a great job. The normal person isn't out there seeing what I do. When I'm 75 and my grandkids come to me and ask questions, I'll be able to say I was there and I was the police."

Yet, being the police comes with its share of challenges, both on and off the job. When crime hits its high mark in the 25th District, Kumiega is forced into additional action, his presence, along with that of other district officers, a necessity.

"Now, you're out patrolling the area more aggressively because you know there's tension between those gangs. Normally, you're heading off the streets at 1 A.M., but now you're out to 1:30 or 2:00 A.M. You come across a guy with a pistol and it's another hour to get in the station. Then, you have another four hours to ready the paperwork. All of a sudden it's 6:30 A.M.," he says.

"So for me, it's Monday morning at 7 A.M. when I get home and my wife's on her way out the door to work so I only see her in passing. The kids are up and I stay with them until they nap. Counting the next shift that I begin at 6 P.M., I've been up 48 hours with only a four-hour nap right in the middle. But then I have to realize that this is the job I chose. And I have to remind myself of the good that can come of this work."

Though his stubbled face and husky frame offers the appearance of a rugged, no-nonsense fellow, Kumiega remains a man rooted in family values and patience. In his daily chase of the 25th District's gang hierarchy, he attempts to understand crime and the people involved in it.

"You look at the guys who hang out on the corner day after day, the constant turmoil and drama in their lives. You wonder, 'What's the attraction? What drew them to that lifestyle?' There's a time out there when you'll actually talk to the gang member as a buddy—you actually have a normal conversation—and you try to understand what's going on in their mind. But you always know how quickly it can change. You realize there's a fine line on the streets between being a criminal and being the police."

A cop's overall view of humanity can often nosedive as well, given that an officer lives in full recognition of the crime that fills Chicago's streets.

"When you're out on the streets you see what can happen to anyone at any time. You sometimes expect the worst in situations," Kumiega says. "I'll drive home and see a suspicious car ahead, so I slow down. I make sure the doors are locked, a light's on, change my route home, and change up my schedule. When I come to a stoplight, I look in my mirrors. The mentality is that anything can happen to me—and that's entirely a product of seeing what happens on a daily basis."

For Kumiega, an uneasy feeling resonates, and it's one he sometimes wishes he could live without. For many Chicago Police officers, the awareness of the criminal element sparks concerns that rarely consume the average citizen's mind.

"It does scare me a bit that I live in this world of 'what ifs.' It doesn't terrify me, but it does put me on edge," he says. "You're playing all these scenarios through your mind and contemplating solutions. You're going over the drills in your mind so you know what to do in the event that something does happen.

"Part of me wishes I could live like a dentist. The dentist doesn't think about a carjacking or a home invasion because those things are not a part of his world; he doesn't witness them firsthand. But my world knows these things are out there and so I am prone to think about them more often."

Perhaps no day reminded Kumiega that his professional life and personal life could collide more so than the day he responded to an armed robbery call at a Northwest Side clothing store. There, he found his mother in tears. A cashier at the store, she was the victim.

"A guy had come in and put a gun right to her face," says Kumiega. "I was immediately overcome with rage, but that rage was also tied up with joy that she was ok. Normally, you get to a scene and need to act objectively. When you see something like that happen though, it eats you up inside."

Yet in a strange irony, Kumiega says he achieves a sense of sure footing amid the turbulence. Living the life of a frontlines officer, rarely shielded from the immediacy of crime, he feels that he emerges as a more complete human being.

"Take an event in which you see something done to a kid. You're even more anxious to get home and see your own children and hug them," he says. "You're thankful you're raising them the way you are. A few times I've come home and just sat in my kids' bedroom as they've slept and thought about what not to do as a parent. In a strange way, it almost inspires you.

"Something else about being a cop, it teaches you how to deal with anger," he continues. "You're dealing with so much negativity, so many people who disrespect themselves and life, that you're learning how not to live. It shows you how to be a better person because you're constantly seeing all these negative actions around you."

> ➤ *Area 5 Headquarters on the city's Northwest Side (Grand and Central) also hosts the 25th Police District, one of the city's most diverse and expansive districts. Until his recent move into the citywide Gang Intelligence Unit, Officer Dave Kumiega had spent his entire career in the 25th District.*
> Courtesy of Daniel P. Smith

Despite hopes that his city wasn't so penetrated by crime, Kumiega relishes his opportunities to diminish Chicago's criminal impact. Though he speaks of a decrease in time with his family, an inability to get to Wrigley Field for a game, and the unforgiving toll that the job inflicts on his personal health, his words seamlessly shift to detail an unrelenting passion for the job, his desire to see Chicago's citizens pleased with their police efforts, and the consistent energy that dominates his work.

"There's so much activity in Chicago that you can sit on one spot and get a pistol, climb into an abandoned building and watch a dope spot, or turn a corner and see a shooting," he says. "In Chicago, there's always something going on. It might be the dead of winter, but there's still drugs being moved. Gangs don't go into hibernation. And I love being out on the street and tracking the bad guys down. I love that adrenaline rush.

"A lot of the old timers will tell you to do what's best for your family. Maybe you take an advance for a raise or a different position with less legwork. But when I sit down and think about it these days, when I think about it for my family, I see it differently. I see myself making things better for them and I'd hope all of Chicago's officers would be as committed to that goal. If we're aggressive in making things better and safer for our own families, then that will make things better for the city."

Now, as midnight approaches in his own home, Kumiega sits in his basement looking at a collection of his children's toys and photos. He ate dinner in under 10 minutes this evening, putting his oldest son on his lap as he pulled bites of food to his mouth. After a late arrest, he had again told his wife to go on with dinner; he'd get home as soon as he could.

"I'll have some people tell me to take it easy, scale back," he says, "but that isn't the work I signed on to do. I'm a police officer and I'm always supposed to be doing something.

"Maybe I'll wish for the dentist's life every once in a while, but I still know deep down that I'm supposed to be the police."

SHOTS FIRED:
DETECTIVE MIGUEL RIOS

———————————————★———————————————

Miguel Rios had it—even as a youngster. The sense that something was awry and he needed to act.

Growing up in Chicago's Back of the Yards neighborhood, Rios said he saw it all—gun fights, brutal beatings, robbery, and drugs. And somehow, in the middle of the chaos, Rios kept walking the straight line, kept his eyes focused ahead. Perhaps it was his working parents, who provided strong values for eight children, or maybe it was his five older siblings, who made their kid brother stay straight. Whatever it was, Rios served as a self-appointed neighborhood cop. He broke up auto burglaries and beatings and chased down criminals long before he received a star and took an oath.

Rios tells about one early morning when he and his brother awoke to sounds outside their front door. His brother grabbed a baseball bat and Miguel slid into shoes. The pair headed upstairs. They opened the front door to see two teens breaking into a car. Miguel then chased them in one of the many instances when he thwarted crime with little more than instinct and intensity.

So when the police test came up, it was a mere formality for Miguel Rios. It was already inside him. Already present. That knack. That passion. That sixth sense that he could do things that maybe others couldn't. Possessing a will that maybe others couldn't or wouldn't match.

"I didn't know I was gonna be the police," he says.

And when the most dangerous work presented itself, Rios answered the call. No matter how great his fear, no matter how worthy his reservations, he did what he always did: he acted.

———————————————★———————————————

Officer Don Marquez's body lay inside the front door, and Miguel Rios wondered what had brought him here, to this moment, to this exchange of bullets between suspect and police. And why, why did Marquez have to be there? He had a wife and kids—good reason to avoid this type of situation.

He didn't deserve this fate.

When the first call came over the radio, Rios and his longtime partner, Jaime Rodriguez, sat at Lake and Pulaski avenues on Chicago's West Side. A "shots fired and possible officer down" call at Altgeld Street and Avers Avenue, directly north of the pair's current position, prompted movement northward.

A "slow it down" call arrived seconds later and Rios sensed that he and his partner would likely greet a sensitive situation. Just blocks away, Rios and Rodriguez heard a third call: "shots fired at police." Intensity mounted. It's an odd thing about the police, that when a "shots fired" call goes out, most prudent people run the other way; police, however, run into the action—one of those "do as I say, not as I do" things.

As Rios and Rodriguez neared Altgeld and Avers, they exited their car at the corner and immediately heard shots. The two took cover behind their squad car, attempting to discover the shots' origin. Ahead, they noticed a two-story home surrounded by Chicago Police, including one—Officer Thomas Hope—crouching on the side of the porch. That's where Rios ran. The homeowner continued firing at police outside.

Earlier that day, Marquez arrived to serve the man an arrest warrant for housing violations. After several failed attempts to deliver the warrant, Marquez returned later, intending to batter down the door. His return and subsequent smashing of the door, however, was answered by shots from the homeowner, who held a pair of .22mm pistols—one in each hand.

On the side of the porch and with Marquez lying above them, Rios and Hope searched for an angle from which to fire inside the home while the man continued to direct random gunshots at the police outside. From the corner of his eye, Rios noticed Officer Roger Forte, an old-timer with three decades on the job, darting toward the stairs, and Rios and Hope followed suit. The two reached Marquez and grabbed his body, one on each side. A bullet streaked by Rios. In moving Marquez away from the home's door, other police rushed in, eventually killing the man. Forte and Rios carried Marquez off the stairs and into the street. Yet, Marquez, who was shot in the head and chest, likely died before Forte and Rios even reached him.

"You give Roger all the credit in the world," Rios says. "He's the one who had the initiative to run up the stairs and get Marquez. He made the boldest move of all. He put everything aside and did his job. But when I was running up that porch after Roger, all I'm thinking is 'My kids. My kids.' I was scared.

I was afraid. Then, once I was there and that first shot went by, all I was thinking about was Marquez and Roger and getting out of there.

"And what really hurt me was Donnie Marquez not making it, especially when I met his wife and his kids—just the sweetest family. I think about my family, and it's a shame [Marquez] didn't get to make it and things had to go down the way they did."

Rios gazes at his kitchen countertop as he relays the events, pausing frequently to consider his words and seeking assurance that they meet the appropriate tone of reverence.

➤ *Among his many assignments, Chicago Police officer Miguel Rios claimed a stint in the city's 9th District. Sitting in Bridgeport, one of the city's most historic and politically charged neighborhoods and home to Comiskey Park (now US Cellular Field), Rios encountered an abundance of action in a district rarely lacking in character or crime.*
Courtesy of Jennifer Sisson Photography

"We tried," he says. "We tried to give him a second chance. You'd do it for any copper. But you start to second-guess yourself. I was down by the porch a good three to five minutes before I saw Roger run up. Maybe things could've been different."

Rios has run that spring night through his mind frequently, each time attempting to discern what he could have done differently. Today is no different as he goes through a list of potential scenarios. He brings his hands to his face, covering his closed eyes.

Self-doubt, it is said, consumes the mind of any officer, particularly with "shots fired" calls. *Did I do the right thing? Could I have done more?* In the case of Don Marquez in March of 2002, Miguel Rios did not necessarily do what he was trained to do, but rather what he believed he should do: run up the stairs with Forte and intercept Marquez from further danger. Maybe— and one never knows—getting Marquez out a minute earlier might have been enough to save him. The self-doubt cuts into Rios; the second-guessing, however, has neither purpose nor comfort. Rios and all police officers live with reality and little else. Second-guessing cannot factor into the copper's life.

The Don Marquez incident does not stand as Miguel Rios's sole encounter with gunfire. While many officers go through their career without discharging their weapon, others, like Rios, get tangled in such moments where the use of a gun is necessary, and life ends. And in no case, says Rios, is it ever easy.

In 1996, Miguel Rios joined the Chicago Police Department, motivated by his upbringing in the South Side's Back of the Yards neighborhood.

"In Back of the Yards, I saw people getting shot at and killed," said Rios, an eight-year veteran of the force and currently a detective. "I saw a lot before I ever even got on the job. All that bad and negative around me, I wanted something different. So when the opportunity came to take the police test, I did."

Rios started in the 10th District in October 1996, a district divided as equally along racial lines—the Hispanics living south and the African-Americans north of Cermak Road—as along gang lines, with the Latin Kings and Two Six dominating the area. In less than one year, Rios moved out of the 10th District, beginning a nomadic police existence that kept him nowhere too long. In March of 1997, he began work in Englewood, the 7th District and one notorious for crime. Rios said Englewood, the neighborhood adjacent to the Back of the Yards neighborhood he inhabited as a youth, never lacked action.

"You'd have some quiet nights, but that's when you'd know it was going to explode soon. I remember going from one end of the district to the other; there was never a shortage of action. You were always moving," said Rios. "And there's something about rain and Englewood. You'd think nothing would happen, that everybody would be inside, but those were the craziest nights of all."

A natural observer, Rios admits he constantly noted positive traits of other officers that he could utilize himself.

"I'd watch and say, 'Okay, that's why that guy did this?' Or 'So that's how I'll handle a situation like that.' I was learning my way, and I wanted to become a good police officer. I'd watch how the best officers worked and I'd take something from each of them."

Following his stint in Englewood, Rios took his lessons to the 9th District, an area including Bridgeport, the famed neighborhood of the Daley clan. There, Rios spent his time on the district's West Side, an area controlled by two gangs—the Saints and La Razas. After a year and a half there, Rios again moved, this time to Special Operations (SOS), a citywide unit deployed to hot spots throughout the city.

"I worked in 10 and 9 and Englewood, all of which were very busy, and now here I am in SOS, a citywide unit that's always busy. Now, you're making your own work happen," Rios says.

There's no dismissing Rios's passion for police work and the city as he discusses his early career. His words joining with moving hands and intense speech, Rios, now 33 years old, appears as eager to tackle the work as a rookie cop. While others nearing nine years on the job begin seeking security after early years amid the chaos, Rios maintains a hunger for more, an appetite following him throughout his career. When he arrived at SOS, the Chicago Housing Authority Police had disbanded and SOS entered the housing projects around the city every night, encountering work that stopped for nothing.

"We didn't want to go home at night. We were going into these unpoliced buildings and shutting them down. The dealers at Rockwell Gardens were practically begging us to leave. They'd give us information about other dealers just to get us out of there. It got to the point where they were looking for us to give us info. You believe that, dealers looking for the police?" he asks.

As gratifying as his early stint in SOS proved to be, his time there also provided his career's most tumultuous day—a day when he fired his gun and killed a suspect.

On September 18, 2000, Rios and other SOS members policed the Robert Taylor Homes, the series of high-rise public housing projects located immediately east of the Dan Ryan expressway near Comiskey Park. Despite having made earlier arrests for criminal trespassing, the officers had been unable to stymie the area's active drug trade. Each time the officers pulled up, the lookouts shouted calls to stop dealing, mocked the police, and ran into the building, which served as their safe haven, given its familiar terrain (to them) and maze-like layout that confused outsiders.

Around 3 P.M., Rios and four other SOS officers gathered blocks away from the building and determined a course of action. They decided all five would enter the building, but only three would leave in the group's two cars. Rios and Officer Gene Bikulcius would stay behind in the building's stairwell to catch the dealers as they fled from the other officers' return visit.

True to the day's form, the shouts went out and the people scattered as the police squads approached. All five officers walked into the building's lobby. Minutes later, Rios and Bikulcius stayed behind to wait for the dealers to resume work as the three other officers took the cars away. They headed up to the fifth floor, waited, and, upon seeing business resumed, called the three awaiting officers on their team to return with sirens signaling their arrival.

"Gene and I could hear the engines of the cars coming. We heard the shouts and we know they're all scattering," he says.

Waiting in the stairwell, Rios heard footsteps. Bikulcius stepped out to greet two suspects, the first of whom was Ronald Terry, an athletically built man with a littered criminal past. With a wad of money in his hand, Terry heaved the bills in Bikulcius's face and ran backwards. Rios, meanwhile, gave chase to the second suspect, quickly catching him and bringing him to the ground. Rios, however, also heard Bikulcius tussling with Terry; in seconds, Rios heard words that prompted drastic action.

"He's going for my gun," yelled Bikulcius.

As Rios attempted to subdue his victim with handcuffs, he looked up to see Terry reaching for his partner's gun and then successfully removing it. Rios jumped off his man, pulled out his gun, and fired one fatal shot into Terry's back. As Terry fell to the ground, Bikulcius knocked the gun out of Terry's hand. And unlike the Marquez incident, in which Rios couldn't save a fellow officer's life, he was able to do so for Bikulcius's.

"The other coppers came in right after I fired and they were all talking to me. I could barely make out anything," Rios says. "And then the whole building comes down on us. They're throwing garbage on us and yelling at us."

The officers called for emergency assistance and help arrived. But for Rios, the thought of firing his weapon to kill another man demanded reflection and an immediate search for reconciliation with his actions.

"You start to doubt afterwards. I was brought up Catholic and I have those morals in me," he says. "When you take this job, you know there's an understanding that you may have to take a life, but you don't know how you'd ever react in that situation.

"My belief is that his intentions were to make a last stand," says Rios of Terry, who had thousands of dollars in cash and crack rocks on him when he was shot. "He didn't want to go back to prison."

Rios confided in a priest and wrestled with the dilemma. Though officers

> *The exterior of the old Maxwell Street CPD station, now the home of the UIC police, was used in the television series Hilll Street Blues*
Courtesy of Daniel P. Smith

take the job knowing they may have to kill someone, it is not a fate many wish to encounter or realize. The event alters many officers' future lives, some visiting a victim's gravesite to pray and others to urinate—each in its own way a ceremonious recognition of living a life in the aftermath of death.

"Taking a life, it was hard then and it's hard now. It's still on my mind. I don't talk about it. I don't brag about it. It happened—that's all." Regardless of Terry's criminal past and Rios's belief that Terry intended to make a last stand, Rios struggled to find solace with his actions. Terry was somebody's son, somebody's father.

"When I saw his mom in the courtroom and his oldest son, I wanted to go to them and tell them I was sorry. Maybe other coppers wouldn't feel that way, but I did. You're taught growing up that you're not supposed to take a life, and I feel like I played God."

Immediately after the shooting, Rios endured the roundtable late in the evening. There, the Office of Professional Standards, the state attorney's office, civilian advocacy groups, and top police personnel heard Rios's detailing of the event. Rios then headed to the first deputy's office to hand in his gun for testing, the standard routine for all officers who have discharged their weapon.

An investigation found Rios clear of any wrongdoing in preventing Terry from firing at Bikulcius; later, the Chicago Police Department awarded Rios the Lambert Tree Award for bravery, the department's highest honor. The award rests on the wall of his South Side home, but Rios's current thoughts remain fixed on the emotion of that September night.

"It's a little easier for me to make sense of it now that the trial is over," he says, "but I'll never stop thinking about it. I'm glad things worked out for Gene. Things could've easily gone in another direction."

In reflecting upon both Don Marquez and Ronald Terry, Rios experiences constant doubt, the consistent questioning that perhaps each drama could have encountered a more positive ending. "In one incident," he says, "I was able to save a copper's life, but in the other it didn't work out that way."

Both sincere and modest in his words, Rios appears to savor the adrenaline of the day while simultaneously seeking comfort in the reality of each outcome. His voice sounds intense at one moment and somber the next, fitting for a man pushed by an innate desire for police work and yet reflective of his work's role in the human experience. In his new position as detective, he admits to feeling lost. He wears a suit to work, has others bring the crime to him, and misses the immediacy of street work.

"Yeah, I miss the streets," he says before mentioning a trio of foot chases endured despite his new professional status. "When I get down time, my partner and I go to hot spots and then call in the district police when we find something."

And in typical Rios fashion, he acknowledges the intrinsic force that has driven his life—the need to act that has survived from his boyhood days in Back of the Yards to his current position with a Chicago Police star.

"As long as I'm with the Chicago Police Department, that excitement will always be out in front of me and I'll be chasing it. I suppose I'll have to deal with everything else as it comes. That's all you can really do anyway."

STEPPING STONES:
OFFICER C.K. ROJAS

————————————————★————————————————

While C.K. Rojas relays the story of his grandfather's life, there's a sense that the tale has shaped the man C.K. has become. Though he never met his grandfather, a law enforcement agent in Puebla, Mexico, Rojas has heard the story enough to know he has a legacy to uphold.

As the story goes, one day, after noticing a skirmish on the side of the road that involved his own son, Rojas's grandfather pulled over and attempted to establish peace. Fighting, he said, was no way to solve problems. Yet, as Rojas's grandfather drove away, the other man approached the car and fired fatal shots into the vehicle. Rojas would never know his grandfather. Today, as Rojas relays the story, there's a vibrancy in his narrative, giving a sense that he's fulfilling a duty to his grandfather in both telling the story and leading the life he does.

"You know," says Rojas, "I always think about how my grandfather would be proud that I'm a police officer, that I didn't let his death deter me from being on the right side of the law. But all I can do is imagine and feel his pride."

————————————————★————————————————

Nicknamed the "City of Angels," Puebla, Mexico, is a city of 1.3 million sitting 80 miles southeast of Mexico City. Puebla is where C.K. Rojas's story begins. New Bern, North Carolina, the birthplace of Pepsi Cola, claims nearly 24,000 residents. A blue-collar town, New Bern is where C.K. Rojas's story continues. Chicago, Illinois, the persevering Midwestern city with a gritty character, hosts C.K Rojas's story today—a narrative with its pen still to the page, the final chapter far from completion; Chicago is where Rojas has found his life's most pressing work, his life's most ardent call to duty.

Rojas, a 31-year-old Mexican immigrant, is a United States Marine veteran, a former cop in New Bern, and a second-year Chicago Police officer. His story is one of progression, of a gradual move from one world to another and yet another with competing lessons, an evolving life philosophy, and a passion to meet his potential. His journey encompasses all that humanity pushes our way—joy and pain, loss and gain, violence and peace. And in his two years with the Chicago Police Department, the work has confirmed Rojas's desire to live life, echoing Emerson's words that a simple existence, merely forcing breaths in and out, will not suffice.

"I want to be somewhere and be active. I want to live life, experience it, so I know what it's like," says Rojas. "I don't want to hear stories. I want to live them firsthand. The police department allows me to live this life and see all of its color, every aspect there is."

Rojas speaks in clear language with his broad shoulders upright. His sturdy hands join often, at once a sign of reverence and at another, power. In one moment, with his hands gently folded in front of him, Rojas contemplates the far-reaching effects of his actions as a Chicago Police officer. Later, Rojas will bring his hands together to match the intensity of a story, providing a soundtrack to the oral history he shares. As a child, he navigated through two worlds, moving from his birthplace home in Puebla, Mexico, to a different existence on Chicago's Northwest Side. Rojas traveled back and forth throughout his childhood years, from a community steeped in Mexican traditions and language to another community with myriad faces and voices. All the while, C.K. Rojas understood where he wanted to be.

"When I was a kid here in Chicago, I knew the fame of the Chicago Police Department was grandiose throughout the country, so much so that the people here in Chicago didn't appreciate it," he says. "And even as a kid, I wanted to be a part of that history."

At 24, Rojas, who left Chicago at age 12 to return to Puebla, acquired his green card and joined the United States Marine Corps. In 1999, he endured a stint in Kosovo, a nation torn by internal fighting and poverty, and emerged more empathetic, more determined. After five years with the Marine Corps, Rojas departed with lessons in hand that would lay the foundation for his work in Chicago.

"The main thing I learned in the Marine Corps that applies everywhere is the idea of taking care of your troops," he says. "You know, taking care of the people next to you. And it's the same as police work here in Chicago. We're all out here doing the same kind of work, risking our lives more than the average citizen and it's important that we all understand that.

"While I was in Kosovo," he continues, "I realized violence and bringing its end had nothing to do with color or creed. One thing that always amazed me was a group coming together to do work, working overtime without a thought, and getting the job done—just for bragging rights, just so we could say, 'Mission accomplished.'"

Rojas's 2002 exit from the Marines led him to his first stint in law enforcement, a move to New Bern, North Carolina, as a patrol officer. Although it's a town populated with numerous retirees, both military and civilian, Rojas recalls a community with the same type of crimes that he would later find in Chicago—minus the volume. Guns, thefts, burglaries, and assaults all made appearances, he says, although they were often concentrated in specific areas of the city.

"[New Bern] was the type of town you'd look at and wouldn't imagine would have such crime, but at times you could get the same amount of calls as you would in Chicago."

For Rojas, New Bern carried its own set of interesting tales. While working a holiday security task force at the local Wal-Mart amid the post-Thanksgiving shopping traffic, Rojas noticed a car in the distance revving its tires and driving recklessly in the crowded parking lot. After stopping the man and running his license, Rojas found the man claimed three felony warrants from Texas—with burglary, theft, and child molestation charges all pending. As Rojas walked the man back to his squad car, the man was, in Rojas's words, "the nicest guy in the world and completely compliant."

Soon, the man, who stood all of 5'3" and 130 pounds, pushed Rojas aside, ran back to his truck, and shut the door. Rojas came from over the driver's side window with his feet on the entry board while his partner wiggled into the truck's cab. The man, however, had managed to put the car in drive and begin an adventure for himself, his passenger, Rojas and his partner, as well as onlookers.

With Rojas's partner inside the truck cabin attempting to subdue the man, Rojas balanced on the side of the truck with one arm over the window. While he considered firing a shot at the man, Rojas dismissed that thought, as he could not shoot without fear of hitting his partner as well. Not until the truck hit a trailer did the chase halt.

"The man was still fighting with us as he got out of the truck," recalls Rojas, "and that is when his female passenger took off running. We caught her quick and she had warrants for all the same things he did. The child molestation warrant . . . that came from the abuse of her own daughter."

Such adrenaline-inducing incidents in New Bern aside, Rojas still wanted more action and the opportunity to increase his knowledge about law enforcement, the chance to taste this world's full menu of offerings. A journey to Chicago, once his hometown, offered the fast-paced action he truly desired; what's more, a position with the Chicago Police Department would etch his name within the mystique of the nation's second-largest police force, his ambition since childhood.

"New Bern took me to a point," he says, "but I was eager to see more. It was my first window into law enforcement and it taught me very slowly. But it taught me well. In getting on the job in Chicago, I felt I could learn all the ins and outs of law enforcement."

His 2004 arrival as an officer in Chicago came with a surprise. To borrow Rojas's metaphor, he thought he was walking into Best Buy and ended up in Rick's Corner Electronics. As it turned out, Chicago was not the pinnacle of cutting-edge police work that he had envisioned.

"I thought I was coming to a department really advanced in technology, weaponry, and equipment," he says. "But when I got here, I said, 'Damn, we're pretty historic.'"

Still, Rojas quickly learned that he joined a department steeped in both tradition and strong police practice. Out of the police academy, he was assigned to the West Side's 11th District, one of Chicago's most crime-ridden districts. Each day, he says, provided a learning experience, a chance to gain street knowledge from the department's more experienced officers.

"Chicago is old-fashioned policing. It's learning from the old-timers and those with more experience. You get trained in the academy, but there's also a street way. If you're not smart and persistent enough, then guys can get away with things," he says. "I've learned more from my fellow officers than I'll ever learn in a classroom. That's the essence of working in a tough district."

Rojas says his previous experience as both a Marine and New Bern Police officer allowed him to absorb the Chicago criminal landscape more quickly. He understood his role, expectations, and the thrust of what exists in the world.

"For a lot of the guys who come out of the academy, they're immediately thrown into a lion's den. It could've been a culture shock for me as a rookie in [the 11ᵗʰ District], but I was pumped up and ready to go. I wasn't apprehensive because I already knew the job—yes, from a different point of view—but I had an idea of what to expect and what others expected of me."

The overwhelming camaraderie of the department continues to amaze Rojas. Despite Chicago's size, he says, the department remains a close-knit group with shared goals. "When it counts on the street and another officer needs help, it's impressive the response you get and how the officers react," he says. "There's a sense of people responding so quickly because others have been in those situations or dangers and know that those seconds could determine an officer getting hurt or the bad guy getting away.

"A big motivation for me each day," he says, "is my partner. He wants to go home every day, and so do I. We take care of each other. We have to."

➤ *Area 4 Headquarters at 3151 W. Harrison on Chicago's West Side also houses the 11ᵗʰ District, arguably the city's most active and crime-ridden district. Since his graduation from the Chicago Police Academy in 2003, Rojas was immediately assigned to the 11ᵗʰ District, an area that demands officers consistently be alert, active, and persistent.*

Courtesy of Daniel P. Smith

He takes a sip of water and straightens his shoulders, remaining focused, intense. Pointing his index finger ahead, he shares a thought of many Chicago officers: "The guy can get away with his crime in court, but on that day he needs to get put away. We need to do our part to make sure that happens."

He then shares pride in his colleagues' determination to consistently battle Chicago's crime, particularly in the face of a big-city media and public often eager to question police motives and actions. This, he says, stands as a tribute to the professionalism of Chicago's officers as well as their desire to carry forth the department's legacy of being one of the the nation's premier police squads.

"Despite all the negatives that sometimes fall against us, I'm amazed that the officers keep coming to work and have such a resilient willingness to be the police."

Sitting at a west suburban restaurant, Rojas takes another sip of water, another deep breath. He's not one to dwell on past events when so much work exists in the present and future. He's eager to say what must and will be done and is anxious to add his own stories to the Chicago Police heritage. He does, however, reflect on those events he's encountered in his brief Chicago Police career, ones that have jolted his life and career into perspective. He begins speaking of a night two weeks into his stint in the 11th District, a call that found him joining a foot pursuit of a fleeing offender.

"I got close to the guy, to the point that I could catch him. I remember things slowing down. He went for his waistband and then he did one of these NBA deals," says Rojas, mimicking an Abdul-Jabbar skyhook. "I said to myself, 'Did he just throw a gun?'"

The offender apprehended shortly thereafter, Rojas climbed over a fence and discovered a black revolver. The man had indeed tossed a gun as Rojas and others gave chase. The event, one all too common on Chicago's streets, unnerved Rojas.

"I remember thinking to myself, 'Man, I was so close to this guy and had no idea he had a gun.' I think there's a point where I'm grateful to him for not shooting at me and the others."

Rojas looks away for a moment, staring into an empty suburban parking lot at nightfall. For a man little over a year into his Chicago Police career, Rojas has assembled a few of the job's necessary traits—reflection, perspective, and commitment among them. He presses his hands around a glass of water but doesn't lift it.

"When you're a rookie," he says, "there's this tunnel vision. You're not looking at the big picture and noticing all the small details before you. I went home that night and realized that I probably should've thanked the guy for not shooting me.

"It's one of those things: It can either scare you to death or you become what you're supposed to be—the police. That's your job and you do what you're supposed to do. You signed up for a specific job and even before you take that first step you know what it entails. You hit the street and you know what's out there. Maybe there will be another day when I get scared or think this job isn't for me, but for now, I'll just keep doing my job. I'm not going to back off."

At age 31, Rojas reflects on the interesting path his life has taken. From Puebla to Chicago to New Bern and then back to Chicago. He recognizes that each place held its unique purpose, its way to contribute to his life's work and mission. Now settled into his work as a Chicago Police officer, Rojas remains pleased with where he stands today—a small part of Chicago's fabled department.

"Everything is a stepping stone," he says. "I started out as a civilian and I had little sense of discipline." I went into the Marine Corps and it shaped me; it taught me discipline, attention to detail, and defending one's beliefs. I progressed to being a cop in New Bern and I transferred those ideas.

"And then I wanted to come back to my roots in Chicago. New Bern enabled me to be a better officer in Chicago. And at this point in my career, this is where I want to be."

Continuing to wrap his hands around the water glass, Rojas couples a deep sigh with a nod of the head. He releases his grip from the glass, knocks his knuckles on the table, and rests back in his seat, his hands soon falling to his side.

"Now," he says, "I need to start thinking of backup plans, because you never know what can happen on this job and how it will affect you. You never know what the future holds."

LEAVING THE JOB BEHIND:
FORMER OFFICER ART HANNUS

──────────────────── ★ ────────────────────

Arthur J. Hannus was murdered as he stumbled off a Chicago streetcar in 1924; he died in the arms of his wife on 69ᵗʰ Street, just steps away from his home. His assailants, a pair of 17-year-old African-American youths, were chased, caught, and chained to a lamppost. Tthe crowd yelled "Lynch 'em" as bedlam commanded the South Side street.

Chicago Patrolman George McClellan appeared on the scene, firing gunshots into the air to calm the crowd. Though unorthodox, Officer McClellan's actions prevented the teenagers from dying right there. A Chicago newspaper report from August 3, 1924, reads, "[Patrolman McClellan] fired several shots into the air to frighten the would-be lynchers and with the help of two other policemen who were attracted by the shooting, managed to take them away from the crowd." [1]

Flash ahead to 1974, again on 69ᵗʰ Street, to find Arthur J. Hannus III, himself a Chicago Police officer. A suspected criminal in the back of Hannus's police car breaks the handcuffs.

"I first thought I'd shoot him, but I decided to jump the seat and grab him," Hannus recalls. "But he opened the door and we both fell out at 30 mph. It took my partner a bit to realize what had happened."

And there Hannus, a slight man, wrestled with his suspect on the pavement, Hannus's gun lost in the fall from the moving car. Freeing himself from the suspect and gaining hold of his gun, Hannus told his partner Tom Farrell, who was struggling to hold on to the offender and his own weapon, to get out of the way.

"I'm gonna shoot him," he screamed.

But no shots were fired.

"After hitting my head on the pavement, my good judgment just wasn't there. And it's the good and right thing that I didn't shoot," Hannus said. "You used to only get awards for shooting people, but sometimes I think the best police work happens during the time in which you don't shoot."

As Hannus shares this 30-year-old story, he shakes his head and releases soft, genuine chuckles. Long removed from his job with the Chicago Police and now a successful businessman, the irony of a story over three decades old continues for Hannus.

"Think of this," he says, "in 1924 on 69th Street, Arthur I bites the dust. Nearly 50 years to the day—yes, the day—Arthur III survives on the same street."

And Hannus takes the irony a step further.

"It was actually a fine hour for the CPD when Officer McClellan fired those shots into the air and took those boys away from that crowd. They could've easily lynched them right there. And, maybe in a similar way, it's a good thing my head recovered quickly from hitting the pavement. It was a fine hour for the CPD that I didn't follow my immediate instinct."

---★---

Art Hannus sits in a corner office these days and knocks on wood frequently, a simple recognition that luck has followed him, with hope that the good will pushes well into the future.

It's hard to believe that a man who had both grandfathers murdered, both parents die by the time he was 19, and a man who had a multimillion-dollar company snatched from under his command, could possibly be grateful. Hard to believe that Hannus, who's been shot at and stabbed, who's struggled with a childhood of poverty and observed firsthand the seedy element of life, could possibly be thankful. But he's anything but angry and bitter. Each holiday season, Hannus hosts what he calls "A Bailey Party," assembling the folks who have helped him along the way. Leaning against a wall in his office is evidence of his annual winter party: a black and white poster-sized sign that reads, "Welcome to Bedford Falls," the fictional town's main street hovering in the background.

"For years, I hated the movie *It's a Wonderful Life,* but I think I get what it means now," he says of the Frank Capra–Jimmy Stewart classic. And of all the things Hannus remains grateful for, one is the Chicago Police Department, the source of great fun, he says, for 13 years. "I loved my job," says Hannus of his years with the Chicago Police. "I loved everything about it."

After beginning as an unarmed cadet in 1967 when he was 19, Hannus became a patrolman at the age of 21. By 23, he was a burglary detective. "I never contemplated being a police officer," he says. "In fact, some of my relatives may have even turned in their graves when I joined the force." But in 1981, after 13 years on the job, Hannus, who had been moved to the bomb and arson unit against his wishes, walked into his sergeant's office, dropped his bag of equipment on the desk, and said he was done.

"I have no reverse gear, so once I was gone, I was gone," says Hannus of his swift resignation. "But I had a few concerns, namely financial. I had three kids and wanted to make sure my kids were taken care of; I knew they'd have to go to college someday. I worried about the residency requirement [that demands all city workers, including police, live in Chicago]. And I was also concerned that the union would move to the Teamsters and how that would affect police work in Chicago. All of a sudden you're working until 4 P.M. on a case and then handing it off to somebody else."

He entered the private sector and in time constructed a multimillion-dollar security firm. In a swift series of double-talking deals and bold moves, Hannus had the business snatched from his command by a business associate. Left with little, Hannus, a jovial and energetic man by nature, rebounded to create a new venture. Today, his American Heritage Protective Services, based in southwest suburban Alsip, stands as a testament to his spirit, skill, and perseverance. The company, of which Hannus is the CEO, president, and chairman, boasts one of the largest uniformed security operations in the state, employing over 600 individuals.

His current success aside, Hannus owes much to the past. He's quick to administer praise to

➤ *In 1967, Art Hannus began his Chicago Police career as an unarmed cadet and soon after became a patrolman. Two years later, Hannus, a native Chicagoan, was a 23-year-old burglary detective.*
Courtesy of Art Hannus

both the Chicago Police Department and his former police colleagues. "Everything I needed to know about business I learned from the Chicago Police Department; rather than standing around, you find out the answers, the solutions, the issues that exist," says Hannus.

Today, Art Hannus is 56 with graying hair and a comfortable lifestyle. His corner office along 127th Street maintains a classical look with sharp hues of green and blue joining crown molding and polished wooden floors. As he speaks, a book titled *Keep Believing* rests over his shoulder while a hardbound copy of the Holy Bible stands nearby. A pair of Patrick Henry portraits hangs on the wall opposite his desk. Hannus, combines a genuine personality with accessibility and energy. He's animated in his movements, often stepping out of his chair to recreate a scenario from his long-ago police career. His answers arrive with speed and confidence and require little prodding. "If I was born independently wealthy, I'd still be a Chicago Police officer," he admits. "There wasn't a part of the job I didn't love; it was the frustration of being caught in the system—even though you might be outperforming others, there was no guarantee you'd get rewarded for your work. You want advancement to come with your good work, and that may not necessarily happen in the CPD. Plus, there are certain basic freedoms I like to believe I still have, and one of them is choosing where I want to live. "But I'm not asking them to change the system for me. I'm going out and creating a new system for myself and my family. I'm changing my system to fit my needs, my goals, my hopes."

Though he hasn't carried a Chicago Police star since 1981, Hannus admits he still hauls much of the job with him. In his office sits a recent photo of Art with then-Chicago Police Superintendent Phil Cline, the pair shaking hands as they pose for the camera with broad smiles. Not a day goes by, Hannus admits, that he doesn't reflect on his police career, use the skills he has acquired, or recall a warm thought.

"I liked putting the bad people in prison because they deserved it; it was that simple for me," he says with a shrug of the shoulders.

He pulls out his middle desk drawer and removes a key. Taking the key to another drawer, he emerges with a stack of tattered paper and worn file folders. He opens the top file of old police records, his own detailed system of notes, discussions, and dates. By his own initiative, Hannus tracked arrests and court appearances of his cases while also recording both oral and written confessions.

"You see, I wasn't only arresting the people, I was getting the convictions.

That's the key," he says pointing to a lengthy list of burglary charges that ended in justice.

His detailed record keeping came in handy a few years back when a former partner, Dallas Tyler, called him and asked him if he remembered a one-time house burglar, a man now facing the death penalty for the fatal beating of an elderly woman.

"I volunteered immediately to come down with all my records. I had his signed admission to the burglary charge as well as numerous signed complaints," Hannus said. "And he got the death penalty—or had the death penalty, I should say, until [former Illinois Governor George] Ryan commuted the sentences of all death row inmates."

Hannus remains eager to help the Chicago Police Department in any way he can. In recent years, he has worked on the department's annual golf outing, an event to raise funds for Gold Star Memorial Park near Soldier Field, a public space to honor the lives of Chicago's officers killed in the line of duty. Today, Hannus is quick to pontificate on the importance of police work and its role in Chicago.

"Most all police know that they're doing good work and that it's

➢ *Chicago Police officer Art Hannus flashes a grin while peering from the seat of his Chicago Police squad car (circa 1970).*
Courtesy of Art Hannus

important work. Just knowing the police are in your corner is a benefit," he says. "Look, we had no human capital in my family. My grandfathers were murdered, both my parents died by the time I was 19, and there was nobody to go to and seek advice. For the people who are the victims of crimes or who live in high-crime areas, it's a real hardship. They often lack that human capital, those people they can turn to for help. They shouldn't have to live like that. Part of police work for me was to become that human capital for them. Somebody who would help them out. And there's plenty of police officers in Chicago who fill that role."

His optimism and good will high, Hannus offers reflection on his own career and its purpose. He leans back in his leather office chair and, in a disarming voice, begins: "I really thought when I grew up that the good guys, the Lone Ranger–types, always won. The women and children and the innocent people were protected. And I was glad to be a part of that. I was happy to be a part of the solution, a part of the bad guys losing.

"There's also a sense of the group that you belong to and the respect that comes with that. You go anywhere in the country and mention the Chicago Police and people know you're not going to back down. Ask people who the real police are and they'll say Chicago. More than anywhere else, Chicago's officers are willing to go out of their way to protect people they don't even know. That's the Chicago way and we sometimes lose sight of that. We take their work for granted."

As for regrets, Hannus names few. He arrived at his decision to leave the job with care and objectivity. There exists no sense of wanting to forget that chapter in his life, no ill will, and no disregard for the important role the Chicago Police Department played in shaping his life and future.

"No regrets—except that it was fun job to leave behind," he says.

But as he straightens his shoulders upon rising from his office chair, a small regret surfaces. A streak of the June sun creeps in his office windows and shines upon his face. In this moment of being asked to reveal his own wish, Hannus clears his throat and focuses a pair of dreamy eyes ahead.

"Sometimes I wish I could be deputized and take care of something. Just ten minutes. That's it," he says. "Just ten minutes of taking care of the bad guy again. That'd be my one wish these days."

PART 2

TRAVELS: THE JOURNEY OF THE CHICAGO POLICE

★

The entire history both of the city and its police department shows that crime, disorder, and police ineffectiveness have been consistent features.

—Opinion of a 1931 Citizens Report published in
Chicago Police Problems

You should've seen the reaction we'd get walking down the street. People trusted us, believed us, and looked up to us. Our own people didn't hate us. They understood who we were because they were like us.

—Former Chicago Officer Randall Baker in *Battleground Chicago*

No one could accuse the Chicago cops of discrimination. They savagely attacked hippies, yippies, New Leftists, revolutionaries, dissident Democrats, newsmen, photographers, passersby, clergymen, and at least one cripple.

—*Time* magazine report following
1968 Democratic National Convention

In the fifties, you could punch out anybody you wanted. In the sixties, you had to go in an alley or basement. From the seventies on, you can't do anything; some citizen will bring a complaint against you. In the sixties, if you said to a citizen, "Get off that corner," and they said, "I know my

*rights," you could say, "I don't know anything about that,
but I do know I have this nightstick."*
—Unidentified Chicago Police officer in *What Cops Know*

We will burn Chicago to the ground!
                    —Yippie leader Abbie Hoffman

———————————————— ★ ————————————————

In Chicago, it's a star. Forgive the poor souls who call it a badge—they know not what they do.

For many Chicago officers, the star holds special meaning, some selecting their number through tradition and others because of some superstition, but all wearing it on the left side over the heart. Some new officers request the star number of a relative, a petition often granted if the star is available. Others reject a star donning the number 13 or if the numbers total 13. A former bomb squad officer with star number 13, Marshal Pidgeon, conceded he never had much bad luck, yet still refused to defuse bombs on Friday the 13th. Star number 1313 brought with it some hard luck in its early years—Roy Dillon leaving the job after three months never to return, and John O'Bryant dying five years after receiving the star, though only 32 years old. Another star 1313 carrier, Joseph Sevick, experienced the death of his wife, two children, brother, mother, and father all within his six years while wearing the star. Understandably, Sevick traded star number 1313 for another.[1]

A Chicago Police star has even saved a life. When a stickup man fired at Detective Thomas Fallon, the bullet hit his star, and Fallon was saved. Soon after, Fallon lost his star, number 560. Seven years later, workmen tearing down an elevator structure found star 560 and sent it to the police—Fallon's savior returned.[2]

Some stars, however, are permanently retired. Over 440 police stars rest in the lobby of new Chicago Police Headquarters at 35th Street and Michigan Avenue. Over 440 different stories to be told. There's Officer Patrick Durkin, star 1549, who was shot while attempting to arrest a wanted bank robber on April 30, 1931; Officer Oreste Gonzalez, star 6263, who was killed on October 8, 1953, as a suspect in the back of the squad car pulled Gonzalez's gun and shot him; 31-year-old Officer Joey Cali, star 3271, who was killed by a teen sniper as he wrote a parking ticket on May 19, 1975; Officer James

Henry Camp, star 3934, who was shot twice in the head with his own weapon following the traffic stop of a stolen vehicle in 1999; and Sergeant Hector Silva, star 1760, who passed away on October 2, 2001, following a special operations training exercise. Each star holds its own story—of life, of loss, of grief—spreading like a plague among family, friends, and colleagues.

> *The universal symbol of the CPD: the Chicago Police star.*
Courtesy of Jennifer Sisson Photography

And as sure as each star holds a story, so, too, does each officer. Chicago's living officers, current and past, possess their own tales to share, and while some do so willingly, others elect to lock their memories in some impenetrable corner inside. In a police department active since 1837, with characters as rich, bittersweet, and charismatic as the city itself, such stories allow us to move ahead as much with ferocity and force as with understanding and perspective. Such stories add color and character to the facts and events that define one of the nation's most recognized police departments.

Early Years

In 1837, saloon owner John Shrigley was elected Chicago's first—and only, at the time—law enforcement officer when he claimed the title of high constable. Prior to Shrigley, Chicagoans relied upon soldiers stationed at Fort Dearborn for protection. Though ignorant of the law, Shrigley had little issue with enforcement and frequently subdued offenders with his fists and hauled them to the "calaboose," the city's log-house jail anchored at Randolph and Clark. While Shrigley boasted arresting power, much of the city's official power rested with its first mayors, among them William Ogden (1837–38), Buckner Morris (1838–39), and Benjamin Raymond (1839–40). By 1840, calls for a more established police force to handle disorder began growing amid some modest chicanery and disorder. The city responded—first with a night watch for fires, thieves, and drunks and later with a nine-member day police force to manage traffic.

On the heels of the "Lager Beer Riot" of April 21, 1855, in which

Germans and Irish violently protested the temperance movement, newly installed mayor Levi Boone, representing the anti-immigrant, anti-Catholic Know-Nothing party, called for an 80–90 member police force comprised solely of natives. With that, the city council officially formed the Chicago Police Department, a collection of 80 officers divided among three precincts and commanded by Chief Cyrus P. Bradley.[3] Unlike previous officers who wore their own clothes with a leather badge on their coat collars, Boone required uniforms to afford officers a professional look, highlighted by a brass police star.[4] In 1904, the city would adopt a silver star imprinted with the city seal and an identification number, the very image of what officers wear today.

Chicago's early officers used their clubs liberally on drunks and other antagonists to achieve order, foregoing a walk to the station house with the unruly in favor of a primitive but instant brand of street justice. After the Civil War, some of Chicago's finest officers separated from the rank and file by earning detective status, a position solely aimed at preventing and solving crime while utilizing the time-honored techniques of interrogation and informers. Patrol officers, meanwhile, worked 12 hours each day of the week without substitution. Upon hire, officers received a lecture from the police inspector, cloth for making new uniforms, and immediate assignment to patrol duty. New officers, generally drawn from the unemployed, unemployable, and elementary-school educated, received no formal instruction in criminal law and were instead encouraged to dominate their beats physically. While many Protestants viewed civil service with derision, many immigrant Catholics, most notably the Irish, accepted the job opportunity, thereby creating the department's long relationship with one of the city's most dominant ethnic groups. By 1890, in fact, one quarter of the department would be natives of the Emerald Isle.[5]

In times of civil turbulence, including the Railroad Strike of 1877 and the infamous Haymarket Affair of 1886, Chicago officers resembled military regiments, marching in groups and squelching disorder with the baton. The "success" in suppressing such uprisings earned the Chicago Police a degree of positive publicity, including a monument dedicated to police that recognizes their efforts in the Haymarket Affair. Erected in 1889 as the nation's first monument honoring police, the statue later became a symbol of police repression during the 1960s, when student radicals attempted to bomb the statue on numerous occasions. Today, the statue stands at the

Chicago Police Academy, a reminder of Chicago's frontier days and of the simple means the department employed to enforce order.

In 1880, the city instituted wooden call boxes for police-men to use as they walked the beat. Instead of taking prisoners by arm to the jailhouse or rushing to the station house for support, officers now had the ability to call the patrol wagon and later, in 1906, a mounted patrol for assistance. Additionally, officers needed to do a "pull" every hour, checking in with the station house and dealing with accountability for their work. While the call boxes removed officers from the isolated feeling of covering their beat, the boxes also prevented many officers from enjoying their favorite workday pastimes—visiting saloons, sleeping, and "hiding the star" to avoid duty, most often a result of 80-plus-hour work weeks that drained the body and the mind.

As the 1880s pushed on and the city's population topped a half-million, the Police Department strived for increased professionalism, earning high marks from other urban departments for its sophistication and advancement. Superintendent William McGarigle offered police matron positions to women, a job tending to runaways, lost children, and the infirm, thereby allowing the patrolman to focus on his beat. (African-Americans joined the department a decade earlier in 1872, though

➤ *In the lobby of Chicago Police Headquarters at 35th and Michigan, a Christmas tree hosts the star numbers of Chicago officers.*
Courtesy of Jennifer Sisson Photography

their service was restricted to plainclothes.) McGarigle would later host a conference of police chiefs in Chicago, hoping that police would become active participants in social control rather than political chess pieces. In 1888, Chicago began utilizing the Bertillon system, a cumbersome process of inventorying offenders by measuring such things as the distance from palm to finger. Though primal in its method, the system worked in gathering a database of criminals until the introduction of fingerprinting in 1910 advanced the identification procedure.[6] The decade also witnessed the creation of two police merit awards by the city council in 1885. The Lambert Tree Award and the Carter H. Harrison Gold Medal are honors still awarded annually to Chicago officers who distinguish themselves in duty.

By 1890, former Mayor Boone's hopes for a native-born police force had subsided along with the nativist fervor. Though officers earned up to $700 annually, a fair amount for an unskilled worker, public sentiment over the position, coupled with the inherent dangers of the work, inspired many to pass on the opportunity of donning a star. In 1895, the Civil Service Act attempted to legitimize and further professionalize Chicago's police force with hiring examinations, merit-based promotions, and the exclusion of politics. Such ideas, however, ignored the realities of Chicago's intrinsic character wherein saloon owners wielded more power than police commanders. Despite Superintendent John Joseph Badenoch's claim to the City Council that the department should rid itself of political influence, little changed.[7] Ward bosses still boasted influence, and Chicago's officers remained subject to political maneuverings. When Chicago newspapers detailed crime waves and public outcry sounded throughout the streets, police brass responded with mass arrests. Though centuries have twice flipped and a distance between city politics and police work has matured, the department's entanglement as a political body resists full separation. As one current Chicago detective says, "The police are like any political entity—they react to public pressure."

Into the Twentieth Century

As the century turned and Chicago's population jumped to 1.7 million, focus on the city's police department intensified as Chicago's public demanded more of its police force. A civic commission in 1904 condemned Chicago's officers, saying: "The police of Chicago are piano movers, bums,

➤ *A Chicago Police Department patrol wagon in the 1880s demonstrates the traditional setup*
of the day: officers in the rear and a Teamster at the helm.

Courtesy of collection of James T. McGuire

cripples, janitors, ward heelers—anything but patrolman! They have no
respect for the law and they depend on the alderman to get them out of
trouble."[8]

Despite the noble strides of the Civil Service Act, the department's
emerging repute, and promises that politics had been expunged from the
department, the public still saw the police as fumbling workers incapable
of positive action. This theory was not all that easy to dismiss as many
early Chicago officers—working-class, modestly educated men—saw little
wrong with booze, gambling, and tomfoolery off—or on—the job. While
political interference and a general covering of the eyes would linger into
the coming decades, Chicago's police department nevertheless attempted
to move toward progress, stumbling along in its growth and eventually
encountering Chicago's most esteemed and infamous criminal clan, the
Outfit.

Yet, before the likes of Scarface, Big Jim, and Bugs arrived to toss the

➤ A Chicago officer (second from left) stands with a trio of residents outside one of the city's first police and fire stations (circa 1890).

city in criminal upheaval, the Chicago Police Department took aggressive strides to be an efficient model for modern-day urban policing. At the turn of the century, Chicago claimed a police force of 3,300, among the nation's largest departments. The first automobile patrol was introduced in March of 1906 and the department claimed 50 vehicles by 1915. Not long after this, the department began issuing traffic tickets as opposed to arresting violators. In October 1910, under the direction of LeRoy Steward, the department began formal training of its officers in a four-week class at the Chicago Police Academy.[9] With the city's population topping 2.5 million by mid-decade, Chicago's department expanded to 45 police districts in 1918, each with its own files of suspects, crimes, and reports. (While the number of districts would drop to 41 in 1930, the disjoint between the station houses would not as police encountered a system mired in inefficiency and ineffectiveness.[10]) By 1924, work would begin on a modernized police headquarters at 11th and State Streets, immediately south of the city's business district.

Ironically, however, law itself positioned the Outfit and Al Capone amid the top of Chicago's hierarchy. The nation's 18th amendment (Volstead Act)

banned alcohol and stirred the emotions of a city thirsting for its liquor. Though perhaps noble in purpose, the 1919 Volstead Act helped the Outfit rise to prominence as Capone and others obeyed the simple laws of supply and demand—Chicagoans wanted their moonshine and lager, and the Outfit supplied the booze in bulk. While superintendent Charles Fitzmorris favored peace on the streets over enforcing prohibition, his successor, Morgan Collins, appointed by reform-minded Mayor William Dever, raided bootlegging joints with structure and substance from 1923 to 1927. During Collins's tenure, however, Capone ascended to power with a combination

> *Until the acceptance of fingerprinting in 1910, the Chicago Police Department utilized the cumbersome Bertillon method for identification, which included anthropometrics measurements, standardized photos, graphs, and markings.*

Courtesy of the collection of James T. McGuire

of greed, viciousness, and quick-trigger fingers at his disposal. Gangland killings after 1923 began to mount, and Chicago's reputation as a criminal hotbed would spread around the world.

In the midst of Capone's reign, Chicago's cops, heeding the demands of political powerbrokers, became pawns in the profitable bootlegging game. As one Chicago reporter put it, "Almost every cop was taking money. He had to take in order to keep his job." The stigma attached to accepting bribes from underworld figures dissipated and competition for police department spots became heated, some ward leaders charging as much as $1,500 for appointment to the CPD.[11]

While attempting to curb Capone's widespread operations and violence, a regime that would last until Capone's 1931 imprisonment on tax evasion charges, the Chicago Police Department simultaneously sought to address a number of social and departmental issues demanding its attention. As crime in the city rose to exceptional highs, the police teamed with Northwestern University to create the city's first crime laboratory, a move made in part to foster the department's image as an intelligent and professional crime-fighting unit that used the finest tools available. In the immediate years prior to the Great Depression, the department's Unemployed Boys Bureau worked to prevent crime and gang affiliation by finding young men suitable jobs. By the end of 1929, 87 percent of the 27,000 boys who applied for the program found work. As the Depression unchained its wrath on Chicago, however, the number of young men seeking entry into the program, coupled with the lack of employment opportunities, overwhelmed each district's officer charged with handling placement. Soon, one of the department's most innovative and successful social-outreach programs withered into nonexistence.

By 1930, Chicago boasted a population over 3.3 million with 6,700 officers charged with law enforcement duties, the overwhelming majority either born in Chicago or longtime city residents, a fact only serving to further the old spoils system so entrenched in the city's DNA. The average patrolman made between $2,100 and $2,500 annually while sergeants took home $2,900, lieutenants $3,200, and captains $4,000.[12] That same year, the Chicago Police struck a relationship with the *Chicago Tribune* and began its own radio broadcasting system, which allowed patrol cars to be dispatched where necessary. By 1942, all squad cars came equipped with two-way radios. Communication was further enhanced in 1952 as walkie-talkies

> ➤ *A Chicago Police automobile fleet sits ready on a city street (circa 1910). The department
first introduced vehicles into the patrol unit in 1906.*
Courtesy of the Chicago Public Library, Special Collections and Preservation Division

permitted car-to-car dialog and a point-to-point telephone system allowed
the CPD to coordinate efforts with other regional police departments.[13]

Forward from Summerdale

Opening the *Chicago Tribune* just about any June day in 1950, a reader
was sure to encounter a story about a Chicago Police officer. Patricia Leeds,
the *Tribune's* so-called "girl police reporter," embarked upon a journey to
tell the personal stories of Chicago officers and their families. The first story,
titled "A Typical Chicago Cop! Brave, Honest, and Modest," was published
on June 11, 1950. In many of the stories, Leeds detailed the officers' family
lives. The series reminds us of another time, when officers' home addresses
were published in the city newspaper alongside photos of a smiling wife
and children. The stories recount the general feeling toward officers of the
day—men with their own set of faults, but also with a genuine sense of duty
and a shared struggle that engendered respect from Chicago's citizens. In
the early 1950s, for instance, the crime rate in Chicago continued to fall
while the nation's climbed, giving many citizens cause to celebrate the
work of their police department. Somewhere along the line, such respect
(some would call it fear) seemed to wane in favor of challenges to authority,
mocking of officers, and a general distrust of their word.

Officers themselves bear some of the blame for such a shift in public
perception. In 1959, for instance, Anthony DeGrazio, a lieutenant at the

Damen Avenue station and a once-fired officer, joined former West Side compatriot and mob heavyweight Tony "Big Tuna" Accardo on a European tour. Though DeGrazio dismissed knowledge of Accardo's dealings, he was soon fired for fraternizing with criminals. In response, Superintendent Tim O'Connor offered the following words: "It is the worst black eye the Police Department ever had!"[14] (In 1997, Superintendent Matt Rodriguez would resign under a similar departmental rule as a result of his relationship with convicted felon Frank Milito.)

The year following DeGrazio's European jaunt, the Chicago Police endured a more embarrassing and disheartening situation when eight officers were indicted in a burglary ring that targeted local businesses and residents. What's more, the officers themselves were in cahoots with one of the city's wittiest burglars, Dickie Morrison. The Summerdale Scandal, so called because six of the officers served in the 40th District's Summerdale station, not only drove public sentiment toward officers in a downward direction (from guys who harmlessly collected Christmas Eve envelopes along their beat to those who actually burglarized the people they swore to protect), but also urged Mayor Richard J. Daley to take drastic action in reshaping the department. While Chicago may not have been ready for change, Daley, facing a threat to his mayoral seat from Republican Benjamin Adamowski, imposed reform upon his police department. Despite rank-and-file resentment of "the book cop," a disdainful label applied to police theorists as opposed to street realists, Daley appointed the best "book cop" he could find—Orlando W. Wilson, professor of police administration and dean of the School of Criminology at UCLA. The selection of Wilson failed to earn applause from most officers, as Wilson represented most everything the rank-and-file despised—outsiders and academic-minded book cops—as well as being unrelated to Chicago's ethnic enclaves.

While some officers have diminished Wilson's importance, saying he did little more than change the color of the squad cars and provide the appearance of multi-layered change, others argue that Wilson's seven years atop the department witnessed the birth of true professionalism in the ranks, modernization, and leave the beginning of the department's slow break from the burdensome thumb of politics.

As a condition of his hire, Wilson demanded political independence from Daley and soon moved the superintendent's office out of City Hall and into CPD Headquarters at 11th and State. Wilson later closed police districts and reorganized the 21 new districts' lines without regard for ward politics, a stronger move than any superintendent had ever made to quiet ward power over the department. He also sought advanced technology, encouraged merit promotions rather than political ones, recruited university students, tightened discipline structure, limited foot patrols in favor of the faster response times of patrol cars, and encouraged diversity in the department with a focused hiring and promotion of black and female officers. As author Richard Lindberg writes in *To Serve and Collect*, "O.W. Wilson blended scholarship with a hard-nosed approach to law enforcement. To these ends he was a disciplinarian who believed that the police executive should be more than a figurehead, a situation that had existed far too long in Chicago."[15]

After Wilson's retirement in 1967, Mayor Richard J. Daley's "shoot to kill" arsonists order following the assassination of the Reverend Martin Luther King and the uprising that followed, coupled with the mayor's insistence of tough love during the 1968 Democratic National Convention, signalled a break from Wilson's professional, objective tone. At the same time, however, Daley's orders characterized the feelings of the many

➤ *Chicago Police officers (from left) Donahue, Sullivan, and Crowley stand with their primitive Paddy Wagon outside the Lawndale Station in 1914. The Paddy Wagon, still a commonly used term today, earned its moniker in the early nineteenth century from a combination of two factors: its frequent duty in rounding up drunk men in a tour of the city's streets, and the Irish officers who often held the wagon's reigns.*

Courtesy of the Chicago Public Library, Special Collections and Preservation Division

> *Chicago Police squadrons sport the CAPS logo underneath the city's flag. The department's introduction of the CAPS program, a move spurred by Mayor Richard M. Daley in the early 1990s, signaled a return to some old-fashioned policing methods, namely stepping out of the squad car and communicating with residents and businesses.*

Courtesy of Jennifer Sisson Photography

Chicagoans who detested the invasion of outsiders into their city.

As the nation moved through the 1960s and into the 1970s, the culture of America and its famed Midwestern city endured its most turbulent social shift—rebelliousness, challenges to authority, recreational drug use, and street gangs all confronting the status quo. Increasingly, the Chicago Police Department encountered public fire for over-aggressive action and prejudice. With tensions between police and the city's African-American community mounting, particularly following the 1969 killing of Black Panther leaders Fred Hampton and Mark Clark by state's attorney officers, a 1976 court edict forced the city to add and promote more black officers to its largely white department. In addition, female officers joined the rank-and-file as sworn officers in 1974. Nine years later, the city would appoint its first African-American police superintendent with the assignment of Fred Rice to Chicago's top-cop role, a sign of the city and department's swing to a more inclusive environment.

Once again in its history, the department attempted to foster a more

action on public ways) coupled with old-fashioned policing techniques, such as foot patrols and increased communication with local residents. By year's end, Chicago recorded 448 homicides, a 25 percent decline from 2003, while overall crime dropped four percent.[19] In subsequent years, Chicago's crime numbers have remained steady as the nation's crime and murder rates climb. "Chicago's come a long way from the days of Carter Harrison," admits author Rich Lindberg, "but the road ahead is still a long one."

Though Chicago added over 112,000 residents (a population near the size of downstate Peoria) to its boundaries between 1990 and 2000, the department itself grew by less than 500 officers to 13,500, still the quoted number arriving mechanically from CPD headquarters, a new high-tech facility built at 35th Street and Michigan Avenue in 2000. In a time when the nation has been attacked and governmental defense spending has reached new highs, Chicago's officers persist despite the immense burdens thrust on a department expected to secure its own urban streets, yet also to prepare for any of the threats a major international city might encounter from outside its limits.

"Society has messed with the honesty and resolve of police by expecting too much from them," asserts Robert Blau in *The Cop Shop.* "The simple, well-defined role played for generations—Stop, thief!—no longer enough."[20]

➢ *In 2000, the Chicago Police Department abandoned its longtime home at 11th and State Streets (now hosting new condominiums and townhouses) and escaped to the city's South Side at 35th Street and Michigan Avenue. The state-of-the-art facility houses a variety of departmental units, including the superintendent's office.*
Courtesy of Jennifer Sisson Photography

Voices of History

Chicago's cadre of 13,500 sworn officers is spread among the city's 25 police districts and its various specialized units, groups answering over five million calls for emergency service each year. For a city historically soaring in crime and violence, the department's recent success speaks to its evolution and progress. Once a public unit defined by corruption, graft, and laziness, the Chicago Police Department has tiptoed from its negative image and promoted professionalism, service, and proactive measures. Its story can be told in statistics, yet just as easily, and far more compellingly, in the Chicagoese dialect so prevalent among the police department's members.

From the mouths of those who have donned the star, eaten a hot dog at Jimmy's Red Hots on Grand Avenue, and mixed duty with humor come the following tales: retired officer and current fireman John O'Shea, as true a Chicago neighborhood guy as this department and city's ever seen; recently retired Sergeant Bill Jaconetti, one of the few Chicago officers to have a street named in his honor, a homage to his footwork in one of Chicago's oldest communities; current Winnetka Police Chief Joe DeLopez, a one-time finalist for the city's police superintendent post, who wondered aloud what it would be like to call the shots; and retired officer "Uncle Willie" Calabrese, who not only toured the Austin neighborhood's streets and schools as Officer Friendly but refused to leave the job just because age told him he must. Each man has walked Chicago's streets, driven the alleys, met the neighbors, and witnessed the best and worst the city's character and soul offer. Their stories show compassion and honor, responsibility and passion, acumen and comedy. Above all, however, their stories contribute to Chicago's moving dialog about a city destroyed by fire long over a century ago and yet, to borrow Algren's words, still "on the make."

EVOLUTION:
RETIRED OFFICER JOHN O'SHEA

———————————————— ★ ————————————————

It's only 11:30 A.M., but John O'Shea's been talking for a good 90 minutes at a Northwest Side diner. His arms and face maintain a constant animation, his voice rises with each story, and his gregarious nature consumes both space and time. His one-liners emerge quickly and merit—at the absolute minimum—a chuckle.

He's speaking of his 35-year Chicago Police career and weaves humor and insight into his storytelling. He remembers what others call "the good ol' days" and reminds that, given the passage of time, the future will label today the same way. But more than anything, O'Shea demonstrates the mentality that allowed him to survive his career as an officer—a mixture of understanding, flexibility, and a sense of humor.

"You remember the parable of Jesus being on the hill with the adulteress?" O'Shea starts. "Jesus says, 'Let he who has not sinned cast the first stone.' All of a sudden a woman comes up and hits the adulteress over the head with a stone. Jesus says, 'How many times do I have to tell you, mom? Stop screwing up my parables.'"

O'Shea's laughter subsides to reveal the true purpose of his story: to show that it's difficult for a policeman to remain perfect on the job; that the public wants the police to do their job, but doesn't want to see them do their job; and that, at the heart of it all, we're all human. We sin—the police, the citizens, everybody—and the true test of our character emerges in the aftermath. Chicago's officers, says O'Shea, work with crime each day, and the public must understand the delicacy of the situation, how fast things happen, how quickly control must be gained, and how we are all prone to errors. Mistakes happen, consequences follow, but pencils have erasers.

And Chicago, says O'Shea, has always been a pencil town.

———————————————— ★ ————————————————

There are moments that define a city, moments in which a city and its inhabitants must show their true character.

Following the Great Chicago Fire of 1871, citizens banded to rebuild their city from the torched ground. Visionaries recognized the opportunity to make Chicago a great modern city and worked for their goals with such resolve that, with the support and participation of its people, Chicago became a great modern city. Chicago, it is said, showed the power of communal civic spirit, and the legacy of its rebirth continues to define the characteristics of this city—bighearted, protective of its territory, and proud to accomplish things thought impossible.

Nearly a century later, in 1968, another moment erupted in Chicago, a movement that would define the city, again putting its character on display— with the rest of the country and even the world—witnesses to each step.

In the spring of 1968, riots exploded on the city's West Side following the assassination of the Reverend Martin Luther King. John O'Shea, a rookie cop in the Austin district in which he grew up, first encountered the upheaval at Austin High School. Students threw rocks and bottles at the police, who were marching with the brigade of protestors east down Madison Avenue.

"I look back at that event and think it could have been another Kent State," says O'Shea, now gray-haired and reflective about a day nearly four decades old. "It was mass mayhem down there. But this was the whole environment we were in."

The West Side riots, however, were but a prelude to a more global event, an event that permanently—if unfairly—labeled Chicago and its police department. Unfairly? Who knows? It likely depends on which side of the bedlam you found yourself. Were you getting subdued by a police officer's club or were you the target of bottles, stones, and feces?

The 1968 Democratic National Convention in August pitted "us against them"—in some ways gloriously displaying Chicago's longtime tendency to stand up against invaders who seemed to think they were better, smarter, tougher, and able to wiggle around Chicago's law. The city, however, had its own reputation to maintain. There was Mayor Richard J. Daley, a modern urban king if there ever was one, and his attempts to exert control over his city despite a charge from outsiders and the Yippie group exclusively formed for the 1968 convention. Abbie Hoffman and Jerry Rubin led the regiment of mostly middle- to upper-class twentysomethings intent on their voice being heard and well aware that television cameras rolled.

This is the climate in which John O'Shea found himself. A foot soldier in Daley's police force seeking to play his role in establishing the order the mayor demanded. As police officers confronted protestors, the masses pushed their ways elsewhere, simultaneously redefining space and democracy. Chicago, showing that gritty character it did a century earlier, protected its space, marking its territory with toughness. Confrontation resulted between those on the ground directed to protect order—the Chicago Police Department— and those seeking to squelch order and push their agenda forward. Just as the protestors felt they had their rights, so too did Daley believe in his right to maintain order, utilizing the Chicago Police Department as his instrument of control.

Just days before the convention, increasingly aware of the potential for confrontation, the president of the Chicago Patrolman's Association said, "We feel that the insane tactics shown by some groups are getting out of hand. We want the public to know this and to back the policemen in this fight." Police Superintendent James Conlisk, described as "a solid professional," told his officers that their actions would be seen and judged by those across the country. He urged them to act objectively and efficiently. [1]

Like many of Chicago's officers, John O'Shea, then a 21-year-old rookie officer, heeded his boss's advice until the order broke and the semantic issues of right and wrong, reasonable and excessive, compelled officers to act and an observant outside world to pass judgment.

"I'll say this, I'm a man before I'm the police. I have my own rights as a human being," O'Shea says.

And, no matter which side you were on, it was undeniable that the 1968 Democratic National Convention would define not only the city of Chicago but its police force as well. The department's reputation today as tough and no-nonsense stems in large part from actions some 40 years passed.

"We were prepared to be policemen, but I don't know any policeman that was prepared to handle this incident—here or anywhere," says O'Shea. "This type of civil disorder was so brand new. To justify our position, the police department acted in a normal way if you were to get feces and rocks thrown at you. There was no training on how to react this way or that way. You reacted as a man.

"Part of the mentality of the police department then was to not allow disobedience against our office. In the heat of the moment, after taking a degree of disobedience and disrespect, most officers started taking it as a personal attack. We acted like the way we knew, like the way we knew from the neighborhood. As far as human nature is concerned, we reacted as human beings before acting like the police."

Stationed outside the Conrad Hilton hotel, O'Shea remembers protestors dumping garbage, urine, and feces on him and other officers as they stood guard of the hotel's doors. Like many officers on the frontlines, O'Shea expresses frustration at the event's portrayal on newscasts across the country.

"There I was standing at the door of the Hilton and guys are dumping crap on us from their hotel windows above. Ten feet from me is Walter Cronkite as all this is happening. He would later go on TV and say that there were *unconfirmed* reports that protestors *may* be confronting the police by throwing objects at them," says O'Shea, echoing many officers' stance that media coverage was one-sided. O'Shea whispers the word "unconfirmed," his head falling back in a fusion of laughter and frustration.

When the convention ended and the protestors left, Chicago had—desired or not—its defining event of the twentieth century. Its character on display, many didn't like what they saw from the city or its police department.

"There was a challenge to our authority that was new to all of us," O'Shea says. "We wondered if these people believed in the anti-war movement or were they just there to have a good time? We were exposed to something that never happened to a police department. But we learn from our experiences.

"Did we make mistakes? We reacted as others would. We didn't beat for the sake of beating; it was precipitated on the other side. And there's no room for being a Monday morning quarterback when you're the police; you act immediately or risk the lives and safety of yourself and others.

"But over time, I think we've learned not to take things so personally. We've become more tolerant of yelling and screaming, although I don't know how much has changed with respect to a physical challenge."

O'Shea's insight is keen, sincere, and, above all, filled with doses of humor. He knows Chicago's evolving, a young city still learning to walk and stand straight. At 58, O'Shea is in his second year with the Chicago Fire Department, a job he started the day his police career ended, and is the city's first retired cop to join the fire department. He's a true Chicago guy, one who knows his city inside out—the neighborhoods, the churches, the diners, the stories. In fact, his wife's lineage includes an outrageous Chicago historical figure named Bathhouse John Coughlin, the First Ward powerbroker who coined the phrase, "Be sure to vote and vote often."

O'Shea's Chicago Police career began in the West Side's Austin neighborhood, his native ground and, coincidentally, where he is currently a fireman following the steps of his father. "Back to my roots," he says. "I just can't leave Austin behind."

After graduating from Fenwick High, a prep school in adjacent Oak Park, O'Shea headed to Loyola University. To pay his tuition, he worked at a Jewel grocery store on Madison Street until he heard about the city's police test and took it in August 1967. Within four months, O'Shea entered the police academy, much to his mother's chagrin, earning an annual salary of $5800.

"I came into North Austin at a time of change and transition. The neighborhood was integrating and crime was beginning to spread. We were constantly getting calls and the district was so fast moving. There was a lot of rebellion against authority. The Vice Lords were taking shape, but gangs weren't about dope then; it was about kids merging into groups, stealing and then selling the goods."

Within one year on the job, O'Shea encountered both the Martin Luther King riots and the 1968 Democratic National Convention, though he admits not recognizing the scope of the events as they unfolded.

➤ *A CPD squad car sits outside the 9th District Station.*
Courtesy of Jennifer Sisson photography

"You never think of things at the moment. You get swept up in the adrenaline and just plug along doing your job," he says.

O'Shea thrives in the action of Chicago's fast-paced environment, and as his career progressed, he had little desire to move up the ladder, taking only the detective's exam as a shift from his patrol duty.

"I'm a street cop and always will be," says O'Shea, a genuine pride blanketing his words. "As I saw it, when you advanced in rank you risked losing the essence of why you came on the job. You got further away from what was going on in the streets and lost an edge. It just wasn't for me."

In his time as an officer, O'Shea encountered the evolution of a city and a society—from the racial and economic turnover of neighborhoods and back over again to the influence of modern street gangs and narcotics. His career also spanned a landmark case that enforced the officers' reading of Miranda Rights as well as the videotaping of police station interviews.

"Everything was so gradual that it never frustrated me; I just adjusted. We're all creatures of change and we adjust to new times. Today, these changes frustrate me; five years from now, they'll be second nature," he explains.

When asked to reflect upon a career-defining moment, O'Shea steers clear of 1968. For a city, a nation even, maybe that event secures the headlines and warrants the talk, but in O'Shea's world it was a young girl named Miracle Moon.

"Rest her soul," he says. "Rest her soul."

Miracle, so named by her mother because she was not aborted, died three times in the span of a week. Her life, recalls O'Shea, who investigated the case as a homicide detective, was marked by abuse, abandonment, and, as far as he can tell, little loving presence. O'Shea first encountered Miracle when he responded to a call about a drowning victim at Bethany Hospital on the city's West Side. In the room, he saw doctors working to revive the three-year-old girl and, after much struggle, succeeding.

"There wasn't a dry eye in the house," says O'Shea. "But that was only the second time she died that week."

Two days earlier, Miracle soiled herself and her mother's boyfriend washed her off and put her in the tub. There, she drowned and the man pumped her back to life. He didn't take her to the hospital, says O'Shea, because she had welts all over her body from being beaten with an electrical cord. That was Miracle's first death.

Days later, after leaving Miracle home alone, the couple returned to see that Miracle had again soiled herself. She was made to sit naked in a bedroom on her toilet training seat. The next morning, the mother's boyfriend again put Miracle in the tub. He left, telling the mother not to forget Miracle. Upon entering the bathroom, the mother found Miracle unresponsive and called 911. Brought to Bethany Hospital, Miracle was revived; there, O'Shea first met her. The young girl then moved to Loyola University Medical Center in suburban Maywood, where a leading doctor of child abuse reported that Miracle suffered one of the most severe cases of bruise-upon-bruise abuse he had ever seen. Within days, Miracle passed away for a third and final time as a result of her injuries.

Both the mother and her boyfriend traveled to Area Four Headquarters on Fillmore Avenue and were separated for questioning. O'Shea, along with a state's attorney, worked on the boyfriend for hours, seeking information with little success.

"As an investigator, you merge with people and you become compassionate," says O'Shea. "I said to him, 'You kept her under water too long.' He admitted he had and then gave a videotaped statement of the drowning and the abuse. Both he and the mother were charged with murder."

For the first time, O'Shea's voice falls in vitality. For the first time, his eyes aim downward and the table anchors his hands. His speech slows and he stammers over words. Miracle Moon's physical presence removed, her spirit resonates at a Northwest Side diner on a snowy January morning; it consumes a man who saw murder and drugs, violence and revolt, yet distanced himself from those episodes.

But Miracle Moon, John O'Shea cannot forget.

"You know," O'Shea starts, "many guys go through their career doing things, but not many say, '*This* is why I'm on the force.' If this didn't happen in my career—if I never met Miracle—then I wouldn't have much more to say than I did my job and did it right. But I felt I championed this innocence. I made her life worth something. She's with me every day of my life. She was worth something to me. Nobody had defended her existence, but I did.

"You can laugh at everything out there, because it's possible to see the humor in tragedy, because it all encompasses life. A lot of us are victims, but Miracle's story cannot be put into the 'life sucks' category. No copper can ever laugh at the death of a child."

"She should've been a thing of beauty," he says. "She should've been somebody's princess."

In his 35 years on the Chicago Police Department, O'Shea admits to seeing all the city had to offer—celebration and tragedy, brutality and peace. And despite seeing opposite ends of the spectrum, O'Shea has little reason not to revere Chicago, its character and people comprising both its virtues and vices.

"There's an honor to Chicago that doesn't exist in other big cities," says O'Shea. "There's a culture here that says you can help people out. It would be a shame if people didn't know how Chicago works, how this culture exists. If you search in Chicago, you can find a common plateau with anybody that can lead to a relationship. That's why this city's so unique."

And still, O'Shea, ever the Chicagoan, worries about what will come of his city, his department. The influence of the media, coupled with the sheer number of information outlets, places increased pressure and scrutiny on police work. Similarly, O'Shea says, police officers continue to be the lone segment of societal authority that people attempt to control and, in some cases, exploit. This is the evolution, he says, that has taken place with police work. A new era running today's show.

"Growing up, you have your parents as authority figures. As you move ahead in life, it's the teachers in school; in your marriage, it's your spouse; at your job, it's your manager. These are people in authority positions that you cannot react to without facing some negative results. Police, however, are not connected in any of those ways. Police are outsiders and yet authority figures. So what's that make but the only authority candidate you can rebel against? That's one of the major reasons cops get criticized and sued—because people don't have anybody else to lash out against.

"So what do you end up with? You might get PR-enforcing officers who take their salaries and do as little police work as possible. There's only so many times you can get slapped on the hand."

He worries about a new environment that seems to necessitate that officers quietly debate action in their mind while the criminal flees from the scene. He worries about a new environment that shackles officers by providing narrow interpretations of police work. He worries about a new environment of judges letting criminals free on technicalities or pushing forth their own agendas in the courts.

"The Chicago way is being edged away and the result is the L.A. way:

screwing up investigations and looking over your shoulder for a camera," he says. But that alone isn't it: "What concerns me is the people of Chicago getting less and less service because the police are afraid to do their job. Complacency is the worst thing in the world. Today's cop is working within so many constraints, and they keep saying it won't happen to me. If they're so restricted, then cops can't do their job effectively.

"A cop will wonder, 'Why should I chase this burglar down the street. I catch him and he takes a swing at me. So I force him to the ground while some guy is videotaping all of it from a balcony. Then, I get a case put on me for excessive force.' So what will happen with those cops? Guess what, those that have been slapped on the hand too much, those guys trying to chase the burglars and the criminals, they stop chasing. They ask themselves if it's worth the risk. That's my biggest fear: that the aggressiveness of police work will be lost, and that's central to the work here. Chicago is respected so much because it's so street savvy; it'll be a sad day if we lose that."

Thirty-five years ago, in the good ol' days, John O'Shea never thought of such things, never worried about Chicago cops becoming complacent or losing the intuitive edge that has long characterized the department. He takes a sip of his coffee and turns his eyes into the distance.

"But it seems things are moving that way," he says. "And I think it's a shame."

WALKIN' PETE:
RETIRED SERGEANT BILL JACONETTI

───────────── ★ ─────────────

Bill Jaconetti has thinning hair, olive skin, thick hands, and a sharp mind. In three months, his career as a Chicago Police officer will end. And Jaconetti's none to happy about the imposed career change.

"They're forcin' me out," he grumbles. "And why should they push me out? I've been on the job for 38 years. They should tap the mind of the city's experienced officers. Instead they're tellin' me I gotta go. What am I—an albatross?"

Now a sergeant in the 17ᵗʰ District, Jaconetti, a hard-nosed Italian from the city's West Side, will often extend challenges to his younger colleagues, a sure sign that he knows he can still handle all that the job dishes out.

"I still tell my guys I can outchase them or take them in the ring for a few rounds," he says, nary a hesitation in his speech. "And I know I can beat them with my mind. This job is something I've been doing my whole life, so it comes a little easier to me. I know I got more to give."

Poet Robert Frost said all good things must pass. And this too shall pass. Jaconetti's career has reached its end and he will soon move ahead to discover new passions.

"You know my dream," he tells, "is to get a hold of Quentin Tarantino. I can tell him some of the stuff I saw and he's got just the right twisted mind to do it right—just the right sense of how to twist the stories and make a great film. With neither pause nor prompting, Jaconetti pronounces the film's title: "Chicago Avenue."

"That's where I grew up and that's where I started patrolling," says Jaconetti. "Ain't that a great title for a film on a Chicago kid?"

───────────── ★ ─────────────

Today's Wicker Park neighborhood on Chicago's Near West Side is a moving advertisement for the urban renewal movement—posh boutiques, trendy bars, and constant foot traffic of twentysomethings. Today's Wicker Park is young and chic, trendy and innovative. Today's Wicker Park, however, stands a world away from the one Bill Jaconetti inherited in the 1970s.

Yes, Wicker Park—where properties regularly fetch high six figures these days—defined Chicago's shady underbelly not so long ago. Wicker Park was guns and drugs and gangs. Violence and more violence. Dark, dangerous, and criminal. As an outsider, you didn't walk alone—day or night; you didn't stop to ask directions; and you certainly didn't mess with anybody lest you risk a blade or gun at your throat. At one point in the 1980s, Wicker Park stood among the nation's most violent neighborhoods, claiming nearly 40 active street gangs battling for lucrative territory, a place on par with Spanish Harlem in New York City.

A 20-minute drive northwest of Wicker Park on a cool May evening in 2005, Bill Jaconetti sits in a booth at the Big Top Restaurant, a cozy North Side establishment that pays homage to the circus life with its giant carnival tent sign out front. Jaconetti, a 63-year-old Chicago Police sergeant, pulls out a manila folder and begins drawing a line down the middle of the folder top.

"This is the line that separates the good guys from the bad guys," he instructs, writing the antonyms on separate sides of the line. "As a police officer, you need to ask questions. Anytime people, including cops, drift from one side to the other, they need to suffer the consequences. Any question people have about law enforcement, I always separate the good and bad by this line. And I say, don't fall victim to this bad side because then greed takes over. You'll go from being a good guy to being the biggest asshole in the world."

Jaconetti has reached the conclusion that law enforcement, at its core, gives credence to the simplicity of good versus bad, a certainty Jaconetti defines with a thin black line drawn on a folder. In walking the beat of Chicago's Wicker Park neighborhood for over 30 years, a task he left just last year for a sergeant's post, Jaconetti has seen the line crossed many times.

These days, the Chicago Police Department has a name for what Jaconetti did throughout his three decades walking the beat in Wicker Park. These days, they've branded it and marketed it with a logo and dressy PR lingo. They call it CAPS (Chicago Alternative Policing Strategy) and say it's community policing at its finest—an attempt to create a working relationship between police and citizens, making the lives of each party easier. But Bill Jaconetti neither needed the PR blitz nor requested a mission statement to define his work in Wicker Park. He just went out and did it. Each day. For over three decades.

Arriving in the cutthroat days of the early 1970s and leaving in 2004, Jaconetti saw the metamorphosis of the neighborhood, its gentrification, and the transformation from one of Chicago's most brutal neighborhoods into one of its most trendy. So entrenched in Wicker Park neighborhood history is Jaconetti that a stretch of street is named in his honor at the intersection of Milwaukee, Damen, and North Avenues—a symbolic nod to his stature in both the neighborhood and the department.

"Bill was a tremendous influence on this community," says Norm Levin, who has operated a sewing machine store along Milwaukee Avenue for almost 40 years and has known Jaconetti equally as long. "He was Johnny-on-the-spot. He'd come to any crime scene with his own album of crooks in the area. He was always on his toes and you couldn't fool him. He'd go into every store in the area and ask the merchant about his problems. He has a great personality and could relate to everyone. Just an absolutely beautiful guy."

Prior to Jaconetti's arrival, the previous Wicker Park beat cop was attacked by neighborhood toughs and

➤ *Bill Jaconetti began his Chicago Police career in 1967. Twelve years later, Jaconetti would be the subject of news stories and praise for his freeing of 13 hostages and one officer in an armed robbery at Phillips Jewelers.*
Courtesy of Bill Jaconetti

swore he wouldn't return. Then came Bill Jaconetti with the edict to begin locking up the bad guys. Jaconetti quickly marked his territory amid the street gangs that dominated the area, including two of Chicago's most notorious, the Vice Lords and Latin Kings, both in their primitive days, but each still gaining a reputation for ruthless crime.

"What I had to do immediately was establish my ground," says Jaconetti. "Once you do that and let people know you're there to help, then the good people will come to you with info. Even the gangbangers will come to you."

He gained the moniker "Walkin' Pete," a title he carries with him today, from a routine exchange with neighborhood gang members. A teen new to the area asked for Jaconetti's name in a swift, rude fashion, to which Jaconetti shot back "Pete." The teen's buddy, more grounded in Jaconetti's increasing neighborhood reputation, told his friend, "Man, you don't mess with Walkin' Pete."

"They got to know that this was my street and that when I was working, I owned it," says Jaconetti. "I began to know everybody, their nicknames, where they lived. I had my own database of files—one photo for the office, one for me. People knew that if he's a troublemaker, Walkin' Pete will be on him."

From his 33 years walking the beat in Wicker Park, Jaconetti achieved a grounding in a community that few officers ever do. Though foot officers have largely been replaced by squad cars these days, a trend the department has subtly worked to reverse, Jaconetti's work displays the inherent value of an officer walking the street and becoming an active, visible force in the community.

"When you walk the foot beat, you're including yourself in the community. You're sympathetic to their problems because you're in their world," he says. "The foot guy prevents and solves more crimes than you could ever imagine because he feels needed and important to the community.

"All I really needed was to be able to look in the mirror and know that I did the best I could while I was in my neighborhood," says Jaconetti. "Every day I went into work, I went in with a plan, a solution, something that would put the community at ease. Each day, I made an effort to care about the citizens' lives.

All of that makes your job as an officer easier."

Some days required more of Jaconetti and these have become the stuff of lore, heightening Jaconetti's status among a department wealthy in

> For over 30 years, Bill Jaconetti walked the beat in Wicker Park, earning the moniker *"Walkin' Pete." Before his promotion to sergeant and departure to the 17ᵗʰ District, the city and Wicker Park community recognized Jaconetti's work with an honorary street designation at the intersection of North, Damen, and Milwaukee Avenues.*
Courtesy of Bill Jaconetti

legend. He is the current president of the Lambert Tree Award Committee and is a recipient of the department's highest honor for valor. He has received nearly 150 awards for heroism and bravery. "Everybody knows Jaconetti" is a common refrain among officers today, spoken by those who know him personally as well as those merely versed in the stories he tells in hosting his Saturday-morning radio show on a local AM station.

Take the day at Phillips Jewelry, 1429 N. Milwaukee Avenue, the day in which Jaconetti not only escaped death himself but also squelched the plans of a brutal criminal.

"He was sitting right here with me when a call came in about a robbery at Phillips Jewelry," says Norm Levin of February 16, 1979. "And he bolted right out the door."

Upon arriving at Phillips Jewelry that late winter morning, Jaconetti saw one Chicago squad car sitting outside. He pulled off his winter glove and reached for his gun as he stood directly outside the store's entrance.

"I was getting a glare from the window as I tried to look inside and I couldn't see any copper inside," he recalls. "I had a bad feeling about it all."

In an instant, the lead stick-up man swung open the door and put a gun right into Jaconetti's stomach. The fired shot ran through the slack in Jaconetti's jacket, hitting between his raised arm and torso. Jaconetti immediately fired four shots, the final one in the man's ear.

"I knew I had to put on the moves or I wouldn't be around," says Jaconetti.

Though Jaconetti was lying on the ground outside, his work continued. Still inside the store were 13 hostages, an additional two armed robbers, and one Chicago cop. Jaconetti crawled into a gangway to reload his gun. Moving forward, he got within clear sight of one robber inside and, with his gun drawn, told the man to give it up.

"He threw out his gun and I was able to crawl into the store and secure everything," Jaconetti says. "Hundreds of people were there, and even the Feds were there asking me questions. I told them, 'What the hell do I know? I'm just a lowly foot guy. All I know is that guy tried to kill me and I shot him.' As it turns out all three robbers were out on a work-release program from the federal prison."

A far more chilling detail from the event surfaced when Jaconetti shared a later discussion with one of the armed robbers. The trio, later convicted of three murders, had committed several armed robberies in the area, once playing Russian roulette with a Ukrainian market owner on Blue Island Avenue.

"The man I killed was the leader of it all, a real brutal criminal," says Jaconetti. "After it was all done, his own stick-up partner looked at me and said, 'Jimmy was vicious. He slept with a gun and he loved killing people.' The advantage of that situation was that I killed the leader; the other guys were just accomplice killers.

"When I got home that night, my wife was hysterical; the story was all over the news. I made my best attempt to block it out of my mind, but all I could do was replay it over and over and second-guess myself. All I could say was that the bad guy was dead and I was home. Believe me, if there was another option I would have taken it."

Jaconetti takes a quick drink of coffee and shuffles his fingers on top of that manila folder—the one with a thin black line in the middle, "good" on one side and "bad" on the other. He picks up the folder and taps its spine against the restaurant table's linoleum top.

"When I first got on the job," he says, "I had some older coppers telling me I was rushing everywhere. But I was convinced that every second counted, that we were the only line of defense. I think, how could anybody

➤ *In the summer of 2005, Bill Jaconetti's 38-year Chicago Police career ended, a product of the city's mandatory retirement age for police officers. A native of the city's West Side and son of Italian immigrants, Jaconetti had a police career that spanned five decades and witnessed his emergence as one of the city's most decorated officers.*

Courtesy of Bill Jaconetti

tell me that? How could someone ask me why I wanted to respond so quick? Ask those people at Phillips Jewelry. I always said, 'That's somebody's loved one.'"

The gritty side of Bill Jaconetti, however—the side that returned four shots—achieves balance with an equally intelligent, empathetic, and savvy character. He speaks eloquently of the city he loves, the only place he's ever known. He often mentions his parents, immigrants from southern Italy, and throws praise their way every chance he gets. He talks about the respect he has for his Chicago Police colleagues and the work they do, admitting to personal frustration whenever a member of the department falls out of line.

"When I read in the paper about an officer who gets in trouble, I feel bad coming to work. I'm part of that club that's been disgraced," he says.

When he shares his most gripping of stories, he does it without glorifying his actions. They are what they are, he says, before adding, "I hated bullies. I was always for the underdog. But here's the thing, when all is said and done," he continues, "all you have is your good name to protect. And I spent my entire career trying to do that."

Jaconetti's career was perhaps most defined by his ability to change roles in any given situation, to meet the immediate needs of those before him. In one moment, he would play the role of protector in walking senior citizens over to the local store to cash their Social Security checks. Minutes later, he would be the arbitrator, the peacemaker in a domestic dispute. His flexibility allowed others, particularly those in the Wicker Park neighborhood he long served, to see his concern for their troubles and his desire to make things right.

"I've probably worn a hundred different hats in my career," says Jaconetti. "All cops have to change their hats every 20 minutes when on duty. You go from the copper to the psychologist to the clerk to the mailman to the historian to the doctor. Most times you're switching from one to the next and not even realizing it. But it's all about helping people out."

On his final night of work in 2005, with darkness covering the late summer sky, Jaconetti departed the North Side's 17th District station at 1 A.M. to a flood of onlookers. Lined on the street were the district's squads, lights and sirens ablaze, with each officer at attention saluting Jaconetti. It was a tribute to a legend's departure, a recognition of Jaconetti's status among his peers and of his influence within the department's ranks.

"I never saw anything like that and I just thought it was the most fantastic thing I'd ever seen," he says. "It near brought me to tears. And it reminded me that everything I did—everything—was worth it."

DIFFERENT WORLDS:
FORMER DEPUTY SUPERINTENDENT JOE DELOPEZ

──────────────────────────★──────────────────────────

Joe DeLopez will tell you he had realistic expectations, but he'll also tell you he wanted the job. Badly.

In the fall of 2003, DeLopez, a 31-year Chicago Police veteran, emerged among the final candidates to replace then-departing Chicago Police Superintendent Terry Hillard. As the process continued and names fell from consideration, DeLopez inched closer and closer to Chicago's top-cop role, eventually landing as one of the final three choices named by Mayor Richard M. Daley.

Throughout the very public process, arguably the most detailed police superintendent search in Chicago history, DeLopez maintained a straight face amid peering eyes. He told print and television reporters that he was merely honored to be considered and refused to bite on any opportunities to flaunt his own competencies or downplay others'. In private moments, however, he began contemplating the initiatives he could institute within the nation's second-largest police department. And yes, not to be misrepresented, the lifelong Chicagoan and son of a Chicago cop stood truly honored by the consideration.

"I had all kinds of ideas of what I would do," says DeLopez. "You always have guys saying, 'If I was superintendent, I'd do this and that.' I had the chance to really consider how that statement would be finished. To be able to make those decisions, especially knowing that you'd be impacting the lives of three million people, that's a big responsibility."

In October, however, Daley pegged acting superintendent Phil Cline for the post and DeLopez was left wondering about the "what ifs" and "what could've beens."

"When you do something your entire life," says DeLopez, "it's a part of you and your history. How do you say no to that honor?

"But that selection process was like anything else when

*you're competing. You want to think you're the best person for
the job. The superintendent's job is so complex and complicated
that it couldn't have been easy to pick the final candidate. It
was exciting all the way to the end."*

*And with his best poker face and most routine voice in
tow, he offers: "I guess what did it at the end was that they had
Phil and I mud wrestle for it."*

*DeLopez then leans back in his office chair and releases a
generous chuckle, a break from the decorum he most frequently
displays.*

"Yeah," he laughs, "Phil won"

---------------------★---------------------

The Village of Winnetka sits along Lake Michigan, amid the exclusive
tree-lined streets of the North Shore, a place many Chicagoans might label
another world from the city they know.

A town of 12,000, Winnetka is one of the Chicago area's sparkling
diamonds, a suburb where the median price of homes in 2004 stood at $1.4
million—even a teardown, where the home can be razed and replaced by a
more expansive residence, routinely brings high six figures. In Winnetka, the
three governing rules of real estate—location, location, location—apply daily.

The 2000 U.S. Census reports that Winnetka claims a median household
income of almost $170,000. New Trier, the town's lone high school, remains
one of the nation's most elite public institutions of secondary education. All
but a handful of Winnetka's adult residents hold high school degrees; it's a
place where both expectations and achievements are high.

Among its residents, Winnetka claims the late W. Clement Stone, the
founder of the Aon Corporation, a global leader in the insurance and risk
management business, as well as Aon's most recent CEO, Patrick Ryan,
the man heading Chicago's 2016 Olympic bid. International dignitaries,
including the heads of both the Indonesian and Spanish Consulates call
Winnetka home, as do a number of corporate chiefs, nationally renowned
lawyers, and other accomplished professionals. In many ways, Winnetka
represents a microcosm of American high society.

Though not an area where violence runs rampant, Winnetka is not
devoid of crime. As is the case in many affluent areas, the most common

crimes are burglary and theft. In 2004, the village reported 48 car burglaries, 32 which resulted from the car being unlocked. Winnetka boasts a small-town charm coupled with an overwhelming feeling that the community is safe, clean, and orderly. The police department's mission statement sets as its fundamental aim to serve and protect the community, but also to "keep it free of crime and disorder."

Each weekday morning, Joe DeLopez exits his Northwest Side Chicago home and manages the route through the city's North Side and near northern suburbs to emerge at Winnetka's Police Department headquarters. Once there, he walks in, greets others with a smile and typical pleasantries, and navigates through hallways until he reaches a door labeled "Chief of Police." He steps in and assumes his role as the white-collar suburb's police department head, a role he has held for over three years.

In both title and environment, this is not something customary to DeLopez, a man with middle-class roots in Chicago and modest aims. But DeLopez has settled firmly into elite suburbia and its policing ways. With distance in both time and environment allowed, DeLopez now recognizes the uniqueness of Chicago and its mystique-laden police department.

The son of a Chicago Police officer, DeLopez is himself a 31-year veteran

➤ *While much of Joe DeLopez's police career spanned the gritty streets of Chicago, claiming gangways, concrete, and high-crime, his current standing atop Winnetka's police department offers a distinct break, given Winnettka's affluence, quaintness, and low population density.*

Courtesy of Daniel P. Smith

of the city's legendary unit. Raised in the now-trendy, but then-seedy West Lincoln Park neighborhood as well as the West Humboldt Park area, DeLopez graduated from DePaul Academy and then joined the University of Illinois at Chicago's first four-year class. He began studying architecture before settling into business management coursework. After graduation and one year in the business world, DeLopez admits he wasn't leading the life he desired. Despite his father's disapproval, DeLopez took the Chicago Police test and soon after entered the police academy at the age of 24.

"My father wasn't happy. He thought I should do more with my life," DeLopez now says. "He was like too many officers. They say, 'I'm just a cop. I'm just a patrol officer.' They discredit the work they do. They minimize their importance and value. But being a cop is important work."

DeLopez, a slender man with a composed and assured demeanor, quickly shot through the ranks, emerging a commander at the age of 38, the city's youngest such ranking official. In 2001, he retired as one of the department's five deputy superintendents, took nine days off, and then assumed his post as the head of Winnetka's police department.

"There's something unusual about police officers. I compare it to a race horse," he says. "You're always geared up to race and anxious to be a part of it. You're conditioned for that specific work. Nine days wasn't much—I didn't do much of what I was planning to do—but I needed to get back in the mix."

The mix in Winnetka differs tremendously from the daily grind he experienced throughout his three decades with the Chicago Police. While Chicago boasts the nation's second largest police department, a cavalry of over 13,500 sworn officers, many of whom specialize in diverse areas, Winnetka claims a cadre of 28 officers, jack-of-all-trades types by necessity alone. Most notably, the socio-economic gap distinguishes Chicago from its elite suburban neighbor. Winnetka, specifically speaking of size and citizenry, sure isn't Chicago.

"The uniqueness of North Shore communities is that residents are out of town often or in the city often, but they have the means to install security systems or they have folks working in their homes during the day," DeLopez says. "Yes, it's a safe community, but we always need to remind our residents to take the precautions to keep it safe.

"There are still significant responsibilities [for the Winnetka Police]—we have many influential people here who put trust in us to keep their homes and families safe. It's crime against people in the high-crime areas of the city; up

> *In contrast to Chicago, Winnetka is a town dominated by plush greenery and expensive real estate, characteristics that present unique issues for former Chicago officer and present Winnetka Police Chief Joe DeLopez.*
Courtesy of Erik Slon.

here, it's most often crimes against property."

DeLopez's footing in Winnetka affords him an objective sense he could not fully gain so entrenched in Chicago's department. Additionally, his three-plus years away from Chicago, a phrase used lightly as his son, Dan, currently serves in the city's Gang Intelligence unit, afford the opportunity to reflect on his city and career. "You know," he begins, "I'm immensely proud of the fact that I was a Chicago cop. It was a wonderfully fulfilling profession and something that everyone does take for granted. I gained so much knowledge about the world and the social dynamic because I had to fill so many different roles at various times. It's true—the old joke, you miss the clowns but not the circus—because you miss all the people. You take it for granted because those are the people you see every day. But the time comes when that's not the case anymore."

In Winnetka, DeLopez achieved a deeper appreciation for the various aspects of Chicago's department, most notably the resources and manpower present in Chicago that allow it to gain footing as one of the nation's premier departments. At no time was DeLopez's past experience more evident than during President George W. Bush's visit to the North Shore community in 2004, a DeLopez-led task that required hours of preparation and safety precautions including crowd control, bomb-sniffing dogs, and coordination with federal agencies.

"The most important thing I learned in Chicago was identifying the resources necessary to solve a given situation. In Chicago, you can look at the problem, resources needed, and then identify how to call upon those resources to solve the problem. You can put everything together from the inside.

"In Winnetka, the resources are finite and you need to acquire help from others. That's exactly what we had to do with the President's visit. It's days of planning, manpower, and the necessity to be flexible and adaptable. I learned all of that from my Chicago Police career."

His Winnetka office pays homage to the city and department where he spent so much of his career. Photographs of the Chicago landscape cover the walls, as do mementos from his Chicago Police years. A collection of his six Chicago Police stars resides in a shadow box on one wall. Below, on an end table, a diecast model of a Chicago Police squad car sits encased in a glass box. A Chicago Police baseball cap rests on a nearby bookshelf.

"There's a high quality of life in Chicago. For the size of the city, there's relatively little crime," he says. "You can travel relatively safe throughout Chicago day or night and don't have the fears you may have in other major cities. And that's largely a product of the Chicago Police. "I've been to other cities and had people tell me, 'Don't go there. Avoid that place or this place.' There isn't quite that element in Chicago."

Articulate, confident, and dignified, DeLopez wears a purple shirt and paisley tie over pressed black slacks, which conceal a gun near his ankle. He speaks candidly about the lessons he learned as a Chicago officer and admits he loved being a patrol officer as much as anything else.

"The higher you move up in the ranks, the more you tend to lose touch with the public," he says. "I enjoyed being in daily contact with people. You find out that someone doesn't have food or that their heat's out and you get the chance to fix that problem. That's some of the most rewarding work you can do as an officer because you get to see that immediate result, the problem you helped to solve."

While some problems were minor and easily corrected, DeLopez frequently encountered larger issues that tested his intelligence, patience, and faith. In the mid-1980s, during his stint as a sergeant in the youth division, DeLopez investigated a missing child alert on the city's West Side.

"I knew it was strange because this was the type of girl who always made curfew, who always told her parents what she was doing," he says.

The only information police could muster in forming a timetable was that the teenage girl had last been seen talking to a uniformed security guard. Police discovered the name and address of the guard and visited his home. The man provided a likely story—the pair spoke and then she went her way and he went his. Another officer with DeLopez noticed the man's security shirt on the floor and immediately the officers sensed the man knew more than he admitted.

Brought to the district station, the man presented more information. He acknowledged speaking with the girl. He admitted that she did come to his home and the pair listened to music. As the man relayed his story, careful not to incriminate himself, DeLopez and the other officers working the case became certain the story contained more substance.

"We worked him and worked him trying to get him to do the right thing," says DeLopez. "And then he signed a contract for us to search the house; it took a pack of cigarettes—that's it. If it wasn't for those cigarettes, we might not have been able to give that family closure."

The house search revealed further details of the crime. The man had raped the teen, killed her, rolled her up in a rug, and finally placed her under the home's front stairs.

"Talking to the man, we just kept on urging him to do the right thing. I remember asking him if he thought the girl and her family deserved a proper burial," DeLopez says.

"In tragedy, that's what little peace we could give the girl's family. We could give them some closure, some peace, and finality to the situation. There wouldn't be as much to haunt them."

DeLopez shakes his head and straightens his slim frame before focusing his eyes upwards and pausing. For most Chicago officers, violent crimes and the inner turmoil of their aftermath command the soul in the present and remain persistent in the future. Often, the only solace exists in some form of reasonable finality—a conviction, a burial, an admission of guilt. DeLopez achieves only a sliver of peace in this story.

"I guess," he says in a soft tone, "closure is one of the best things you can do in such a situation."

"No matter where you are as a police officer or what rank you are, you're still an important person," he says. "You're a resource for so many people and you're who so many people turn to.

"Who else is there to protect people from the evil of the world? It's not about crime. It's about quality of life. As an officer, you always leave your home realizing you're willing to give your life for someone else. Yes, police officers die protecting strangers. Police don't walk away from the problem; they walk into it. I really wish more people would appreciate that aspect of policing."

After brief silence, DeLopez offers a final thought, sitting forward in his office chair and resting a pair of elbows on the solid wooden desk before him.

"Years ago, I remember asking officers in the academy what they would do if they lost the job? There weren't many guys punching the clock for the paycheck. I don't know if working with the Chicago Police is as much a vocation as it once was," he says. "But I know it was a vocation for me."

UNCLE WILLIE:
RETIRED OFFICER WILLIAM CALABRESE

★

Sally Calabrese loves her Willie, despite all the times he's had her fuming. The couple has been married for 58 years, many of which Willie spent as a Chicago Police officer. The old couple has many stories to tell, each with its own character and wit.

"One time, he's driving me over to O'Hare because I have a flight to catch to Pittsburgh," says Sally, a motherly woman in her late seventies with golden hair, bright eyes, and abundant energy. "There we are then in the car, caught in some traffic on the ramp by the departure gates. What's he do, but get out of the car and start directing traffic. Oh, you wouldn't believe it. Out directing traffic while I'm about to miss my flight. I'm yelling at him to get back in the car, that I'm going to miss my flight. Oh, I was a nervous wreck."

All the while, Willie sits in the background chuckling as the story's retold, beaming with a giddy smile. He remembers this one well.

"Well, what do you expect? Traffic's all backed up so I get out and move it along. That's what I do," says Willie, who spent the final six years of his Chicago Police career at O'Hare Airport— directing traffic, swapping greetings with travelers, and becoming known to all as "Uncle Willie."

"Ten minutes," says Willie, "that's all it took and traffic was back moving. It's not like surgery out there."

"But I was still a nervous wreck," whispers Sally, a heavy sigh following her words.

It didn't matter that Willie Calabrese was off duty. It didn't matter that, to Sally's dismay, Willie needed to get her to the gate. Uncle Willie loved his job and little could stand in the way of that passion, his immovable commitment to his work with the Chicago Police Department.

And after 58 years of marriage, Sally understands that of her Willie, too.

★

Willie Calabrese is 85 years old today, and he's encountering much of life's inevitable pains. He's tired often. A machine forces clean oxygen into his lungs. And he moves about cautiously, one shuffled step in front of the other. Pulmonary fibrosis clenches his body with an unrelenting grip. This August afternoon, he's in the middle of a new antibiotic prescription and struggling with the soreness it imposes. In spite of the physical troubles, he eagerly jumps from one topic to the next: a granddaughter that's illuminating his life; his son Frank, the actor and new father; his son Billy, a soon-to-be retired sergeant with the Chicago Police Department, who was also a lead investigator on the prominent Girl X case, in which a 9-year-old girl was raped and made to swallow poison. He is also proud of his own ability to direct traffic "better than anyone Chicago's ever seen"—the only instance when he throws modesty aside. He tells his wife Sally, "Ah, you hit the jackpot with me. You struck gold." After a wink, he releases thick, warm laughs soon after accompanied by coughs to clear his throat.

He later confides, "Without her, I'm ruined. She takes care of me like gold."

He wears thick glasses, which he removes from his face often, and sports graying hair with black streaks. In the heat of August, he's nevertheless wearing pants, a t-shirt, and a long cotton robe. He's watching a *Law and Order* rerun on a big-screen television in his west suburban home and chuckling at the drama, the Hollywood spin.

"Television," he snickers, simultaneously holding his hand to his chest. "Follow me."

He stands slowly and steadies himself while gathering a long line of plastic tubing into his hand. He shuffles toward the basement stairs. He labors down one step at a time until he has passed three steps. He takes the tube out of his nose, gathers the excess in his right palm and throws it down the stairs. He navigates the next couple of steps without help.

"Every time I go to that damn Bally's, I get sick," he says of his most recent bout with illness. "Fourteen years I've had that membership. Like to go there two or three times a week now to workout. They tried to raise my rates, but I gave them a piece."

When his slippers touch the basement floor, he leans down, rescues his tubing, and replaces it in his thin nostrils. Again, he shuffles ahead, pulling lights on as he moves. He stops at the basement's far wall.

"See that," he says of a lone memento on his unfinished basement's walls. "Got that from the North Austin Boys Club thankin' me for all my service. I used to go there and teach boxing and football on Saturdays. The police department was always good to me, too. They knew I was volunteering my time and would give me Saturdays off so I could be at the club. It was a great place, a real special place for the kids. What little they learned will always be with them."

➤ *Up until the age of 70 and his second imposed retirement, Willie Calabrese, more commonly known as "Uncle Willie," reported to work each day at O'Hare Airport. There, Calabrese directed traffic at one of the world's busiest airports.*
Courtesy of William Calabrese

He points to another memento, one tucked away on a high windowsill.

"That there I got from a fella who was taking apart the platform the pope said mass on when he was in Chicago. Fella just asked me if I wanted a piece and I said sure.

"You know, he'll be a saint one day," says Calabrese of the late Pope John Paul II. "Someday real soon."

He turns and begins his return trek upstairs. After shuffling ahead a few steps, he stops and turns.

"It always seemed pretty simple to me—you just treat people good. I didn't give nobody trouble and didn't see reason to. I just wanted to do good, to respect people and have them respect me. That's all I wanted."

He turns his back and shuffles ahead once again. He removes the plastic tube from his nostrils and lobs it up the stairs. His body slowed, the spirit of Chicago's own Uncle Willie remains as swift as ever.

"It is unlikely that Chicago will have another police officer like William Calabrese Sr." pro-claimed the *Chicago Tribune* on February 19, 1990—and it's true, Willie Calabrese is one of a kind. In 1990, Calabrese retired—a second time—from the Chicago Police Department at the age of 70, one of the oldest officers to ever serve the city and a feat unlikely to be doubled. And while the probability of Chicago ever encountering another like Calabrese has much to do with age, it has just as much to do with character.

"Retire? I didn't retire," shouts Calabrese. "They forced me out. I could still do the job, but they told me I had to go. I definitely didn't retire."

He even bellowed to the *Tribune* in 1990, "I called up. I thought it would be February 28 [for my retirement], but they did not say anything, so I am just waiting until they force me out."[1]

Although Willie Calabrese got a late start to his Chicago Police career, beginning in 1955 at the age of 35, he more than made up for it in working beyond the city's expectations. On February 27, 1983, a day prior to his 63rd leap-year birthday, Calabrese was first forced to call it quits. He took a job with a security company at O'Hare Airport. By the fall of 1984, however, Calabrese returned to the Chicago Police Department. The challenge of retirement ages in court allowed Calabrese to return to the department as long as he could pass a physical exam.

"When they told me I could work until I was 70, I threw the cigarettes away, got in shape, and was excited to go back," says Calabrese, who served another six years until his final retirement in 1990.

"Oh, I loved it," he says. "You could feel like you're on top."

While many Chicago cops glow in retirement and relish their opportunity to escape the city's streets, Willie Calabrese has reluctantly accepted the last 15 years of his life. Even today, he still wants to work—to put on the uniform, attach his police star, and head out to the streets as one of Chicago's own. He still yearns for that familiar feeling of being on top, of being someone others could turn to for help.

"If I was in good shape, I'd go back and work damn it," he says. "I could go back to O'Hare and do traffic. I was good on traffic—used to do the whole airport all by myself."

As Willie shakes his head in disappointment, Sally shares a line she's voiced often: "I used to tell him, 'Willie, you're the only guy I know who truly loves his job.'

"But you're not Willie the Whip anymore," she reminds him. "You just enjoy your granddaughter now."

Throughout his time with the Chicago Police Department, there was plenty for fun-loving Willie Calabrese to enjoy. In 1955, he began his police career as a patrol officer in Chicago's Lawndale district, the Near West Side district then inhabited by a range of ethnic groups, including Germans, Irish, and Italians. He followed that with a stint in the Fillmore Station before spending 20 years in the nearby Austin district, the Far West Side neighborhood that witnessed rapid change during his time there. In Austin, Calabrese played "Officer Friendly," the cop in charge of visiting the local schools and giving talks about police work, stranger danger, and drug awareness.

"I used to visit 42 schools in Austin," says Calabrese. "Ah, they all wanted me because I had this trick I could do with the handcuffs. Used to tell them that nobody could break the handcuffs and then I'd cuff one of the kids only to have him escape. The kids loved it."

A favorite of the neighborhood kids for his sincere and fatherly style, Calabrese would often warn kids on the corner that cops were coming, telling the youths to disperse before the arrival of squad cars. During the 1968 West Side riots following the assassination of Martin Luther King, Calabrese could be found at a neighborhood basketball court playing pick-up ball with the neighborhhood youth.

"It kept them from joining in, didn't it?" he snickers.

Calabrese recalls one instance in which a 15-year-old boy arrested on charges of stabbing another teen in the eye told Austin district officers that he would only talk to Officer Friendly. And so Uncle Willie entered the station to get the story.

"I wanted to help people; it's something I've always done," he says. "I never locked up the young kids unless it was something serious. I wanted them to know that they could always have another chance to make the right decision."

Following his brief first retirement, Calabrese returned to the job in 1984 and took an assignment at O'Hare. There, Uncle Willie kept the car traffic moving in one of the world's busiest airports. Various local and national news outlets covered his 1990 retirement at the age of 70. At the end of one local newscast, in fact, Calabrese looked into the camera and said, "This is Willie Calabrese signing off."

Now, 15 years after his second reluctant retirement, Calabrese reflects on a career that has truly become part of his soul. He never wanted to leave the job and shares stories of his career with a genuine charm and a wealthy dose of winks and chuckles. He tells of standing by "Papa Bear" George Halas and greeting newly anointed coach Mike Ditka upon his arrival in Chicago (Halas, in fact, turning to Calabrese and saying, "I think this guy's gonna be good, Willie") and sharing Marlboros with the likes of Sammy Davis Jr. and Denzel Washington. Still, ol' Uncle Willie, an all-star of the Windy City Softball League, was rarely impressed.

"They were all people just like me. But I always did carry Frankie's picture with me," says Calabrese of his actor son. "I figured what do I got to lose?"

From his police career, however, Calabrese gained much. Alive with humor and charisma, he speaks in a booming voice and talks candidly about his career, rarely missing an opportunity to wink, seemingly his favorite pastime.

"You don't get mad at people. You do good, that's all. Listen," he commands, "if people asked me something, I'd say, 'Yes, anything I can do to help.'

"The police department taught me that I could be somebody, that I could help somebody. You respect people and they respect you. There's the whole ball and wax."

He later shows a police report detailing a recovered purse with over $300 in cash, a purse he found, inventoried, and handed in to the department. The unclaimed money went into the department's widows' fund.

"I'm no angel, but I didn't like the traffic. I was always clean and I'm proud of that," says Calabrese, making note of the department's perception that any minor crime could be handled with a passing of currency.

"He wanted to sleep at night," adds Sally. Calabrese then begins telling of the day after he retired for good in 1990, sitting at dinner with Sally and sons Frank and Billy. Frank looked at his father, asking him if he was disappointed to see his career reach its end.

"I said, 'Yep, I am sad because it was an honor and a privilege,'" tells Calabrese. "But then Frank looked at me and said, 'It was for us too, Dad.' Then, I didn't feel so down anymore."

Again, Uncle Willie charms with that wide smile and flashes another wink.

"Oh, but what a beautiful time," he says. "I miss it deeply."

➤ *Officer William Calabrese tips his hat in salute. At the time of his retirement in 1990, the 70-year-old Calabrese was among the oldest officers to ever serve in the departments ranks.*

Courtesy of William Calabrese

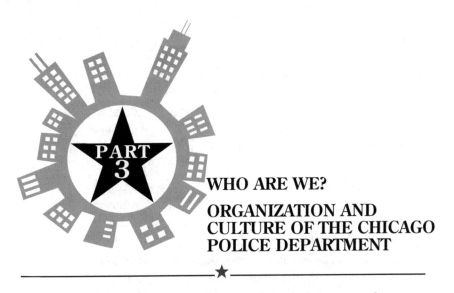

PART 3

WHO ARE WE?
ORGANIZATION AND CULTURE OF THE CHICAGO POLICE DEPARTMENT

★

Each recruit stands up and recites why he wants to be the PO-lice. Some of the answers are the expected drivel: to save lives, stop the bad guys, help people, blah, blah. Some are refreshingly honest: a good way to meet women, because their other job sucked, so they'll never have to get another traffic ticket again. And there's a core group with reasons, like mine, that don't even hint at a need for glamour, glory or grit: families to support, a better way to pay the bills, get the benefits package. Not to mention job security. There will always be bad guys.

—Gina Gallo, *Armed and Dangerous:
Memoirs of a Chicago Policewoman*

Each child has a dream. I had two. One was to be a marine and the other was to be a policeman. I tried other endeavors but I was just not cut out for it. I am a policeman. It is one of the most gratifying jobs in the world.

—Police Officer Vincent Maher in Studs Terkel's
Working

★

We've all seen it—the yellow tape wrapping around light poles and trees and stop signs. Yellow tape that reads: "Police Line—Do Not Cross" and provides a slim, physical boundary to divide *us* from *them*. While the running yellow tape maintains a practical purpose in preserving a crime scene, it equally serves a symbolic reminder of the distance between police and the public. *They* are different from *us* and *they* have an all-access card to the events we only discover in the fragmented details of neighborhood chatter or news reports. One former Chicago detective describes the social split of police officers from the citizenry as living in a high-rise building, the poor on the bottom, the rich on the top, each set apart from the other with only the police claiming access to every floor, witnessing firsthand the issues that spill from too much or not enough, as well as the shared plagues that afflict without regard for class, race, or creed.[1]

In Chicago, a city hosting a police department of 13,500, cops occupy a singular world, one with its own language, roles, values, traditions, and aspirations; indeed, its own culture. And it does so under the thumb of civic bureaucracy—one that imposes certain standards and codes on a public service unit often battling street gangs as much as public perceptions and political interference. Many old timers, and even some young cowboys, have been less than enchanted with the Chicago Police Department and its bureaucratic machinery—meritorious promotions that sometimes reward everything but merit, testing practices consistently tied up in courtroom battles, political heat defining the department's duty, and dictums handed down from theorists and desk cops with little to no experience chasing the bad guy down the dark alley. "Our morale is bad in places," began an officer's letter to Mayor Edward Kelly, a fireman's son, in April 1947. "Leadership can help raise the morale. A raise in pay can and will improve the standards of the men originally selected if the selection is based on merit and merit alone. . . . We have some officials who don't back up the men when they are right [and] are quick to pass the buck and leave the men grumbling about holding the bag."[2] The institution, it is said, is the enemy of the human soul; and the Chicago Police Department can be an institution like any other. Many old-timers sing the following jingle as retirement nears: "I'll miss the clowns but not the circus"—colleagues and the street element serve as a worthier memory than the procedures and paperwork that govern it all and inject CYA ("Cover Your Ass") into the officers' lexicon.

Walking the Blue Line Inside the Yellow Tape

Of all the degrees valued in police society, one stands above all others in Chicago—the street degree. Today's police recruits may need two years of college credit to even sit and take the Chicago Police exam, but the street degree proves to be the only degree that matters much, trumping the bachelor's diploma as well as the MBA. With the street degree comes a set of street eyes, a targeted perception of what's really going on—on that corner, in that house, with that man—a skill generally honed on beat and tactical teams.[3]

Still, not everybody earns their street degree and the collective respect it summons from colleagues. Though some officers slide up the ranks on high test scores or clout, the words of fellow officers—"But he ain't never been the police"—often follow behind, signaling the importance of the street degree for credibility with peers. Others in plush spots may be labeled a "house mouse," a cynical term for those who avoid street action. Some current and former officers argue that today's Chicago Police Department prefers the well-polished, articulate copper, particularly in high-ranking positions, hoping to escape its rough-and-tumble image and offer the public as glossy a look as possible. As such, charge some officers, the "but he ain't never been the police" line has emerged an increasingly popular tune among the rank-and-file.

Despite the recent

➤ *In Chicago's Pilsen neighborhood, a damaged sign from an abandoned storefront shares its space with the Chicago Police Department's latest technological gadgetry, two-foot tall boxes with flashing blue lights and a camera capturing public ways. In 2005, the Chicago Police piloted the camera box idea and witnessed an increase in narcotics arrests.*

Courtesy of Daniel P. Smith

influx of university-educated folk into the department's rank-and-file, a transition that began under Orlando Wilson's tenure and holds today with the two-year college requirement, Chicago, a city embracing its rugged character and championing its toughness, still remains unlikely to accept a department of scientific thinkers and analytical beings securing its streets. When necessary action is required, Chicagoans often prefer as much muscle as mind, as much fist as finesse. As such, the department mixes the brawny likes of Golden Glove champion boxers, such as officers Brian Farrell (a four-time champ) and Pat Thelan (a heavyweight champ who also fought professionally), alongside the high-tech philosophies of Ron Huberman, a former director of the office of emergency management and communications and one-time chief of staff for Mayor Richard M. Daley. The realities of urban policing remain such that video surveillance and computer-driven data provide limited results without a wealth of common sense, instinct, and street smarts to accompany the pursuit.

When John Shrigley, owner of Dutchman's Point saloon, was elected the city's first constable in 1837, he informed aldermen that he need not require assistance in his law enforcement matters. Over a century and a half later, such an attitude persists. Whereas firemen in Chicago and elsewhere live by the attitude, "If one dies, so too does the guy next to you," police officers too frequently succumb to the Lone Ranger ideology and view calling for backup as a sign of weakness. John O'Shea, a retired Chicago detective now with the city's fire department, acknowledges that calling for backup, often the wisest of moves, is often one officers fail to make because of the maverick philosophy that swirls around departmental lore. O'Shea concedes, "No one wants to admit they can't handle something by themselves." Still, many officers, including the decorated Detective Miguel Rios, say the movie fantasies disappeared for him years ago when the primary concern became not the perception of other officers, but rather the safe arrival home of both him and his partner. Today, Rios's approach, coupled with the department's increased focus on teamwork, appears to be the prevailing method, a departure from the century-old demand that Chicago officers dominate their beats physically with the swing of a baton or a sturdy right hook.

Though long-regarded as a domain of white men, the department has placed increased emphasis on hiring officers mirroring the diversity of the city, a process still in motion. Of Chicago's 13,500 officers, over 10,000 are men while 55 percent of officers are white (the city's population is 42 percent white). In contrast, Chicago, a northern city seen as rooted in *some* progressive practices, claimed only 200 black officers in 1955.[4]

While the city and its department continue to achieve diversity in the ranks both with respect to gender and race, it has long claimed a diversity of mind and ambition, perspective, and purpose. Prior to the unleashing of the city's CAPS program in 1993, a survey peered into the desires of cops on

➣ *Chicago Police officer William Johnson poses in a 1903 photo. Johnson was among Chicago's first African-American officers.*

Courtesy of the Chicago Public Library, Special Collections and Preservation Division

the job. Over 80 percent of officers claimed they wanted a stimulating and challenging job, one that allowed them to exercise independent thought and action, creativity and imagination, and the opportunity to learn new things. Fewer than half of the officers surveyed, however, felt a deep personal involvement with their work, many expressing frustration at the inability to see their work through to completion. And while only 25 percent of officers felt management treated its employees well, nearly 60 percent of officers considered the department a good organization for employment.[5]

Indeed, the Chicago Police Department has an abundance of diversity. There are dog cops, the self-serving, self-absorbed curse of the department; as well as salty cops, frequently veteran coppers with cynicism and skepticism piggybacking each word. There are the youngsters "full of piss and vinegar" searching for every big "pinch" they can find, as well as the shifty cops who are monitored by their colleagues.

Whatever their stage, all officers remain connected by the Blue Line, an ideology pushed in the academy and on the streets. While the line stands a firm and unmoving one for some, others adapt and interpret its unwritten codes by situation. Whatever the individual officer's outlook, the Blue Line survives to transcend class and race, gender and religion, petty quarrels and lasting grudges. The Line seeks to drop prejudices and resentment in favor of a unified bond.

"We're all Blue," says officer Bob Rawa, "and that's stressed in the academy and reinforced in the districts. I've seen situations where guys might not be friendly with one another, but the Blue Line transcends that. You support the guy, you help the guy, because we're all the police. Then, you'll see the guys acknowledge that support with anything from a nod to a grunt, though they might still dislike one another."

Nowhere does the Blue Line appear more evident than in the shooting of an officer. Former *Chicago Tribune* police reporter Robert Blau, who detailed his activities as a rookie reporter on the police beat in *The Cop Shop*, says the shooting of an officer always prompted added intensity from officers and activated the stringent standards of loyalty and response imposed by the Blue Line mentality.

"The phrase 'officer down,'" writes Blau, "busted the routine... [in] the street, where you could feel the heightened state of affairs, the cops unleashed, their standards shifting to meet the affront, even in the minds and fists of the smart, restrained ones."[6]

The same Blue Line that rallies officers to defense of a colleague has likewise proven a stumbling block to ethical decisions. When certain coppers fall out of line, from the notorious Summerdale event to the more recent corruption indictment of officers from the Wentworth station in the summer of 2005, the Blue Line often shields wrongdoing officers from internal unmasking. To expose offending officers, no matter how morally correct, serves to disrespect the Blue Line. The problem, say many officers, is not in the existence of an unwritten code valuing loyalty and fraternity, but rather the presence of officers using the sanctity of the Blue Line to do as they please.

"The culture of the department," says one veteran officer, "is such that loyalty is hammered in the officers' heads. We're all the police. We're all Blue. And you respect that because the guy next to you, maybe a guy you don't like, might save your life someday. Still, almost down to a man, all of us want to be honest people, respected people, and valuable people to our city. It's one of many balancing acts coppers have to do."

When asked to name the ideal traits held by a Chicago Police officer, many coppers rattle off the same list of characteristics: physical ability to handle himself or herself, sound discretion, compassion, sense of humor, street smarts, and loyalty to the job and colleagues.

"And he or she has to have been around before they're the police," adds a current officer, noting the tradition of Chicago officers knowing neighborhood codes, who's who, and being involved in an alley fight or two prior to taking the job.

➤ *A flag outside Chicago Police Headquarters, with the Chicago Police star, the checkerboard design, and the Chicago city flag characteristics, emblazons the mantra of the department—courage, pride, and dedication.*
Courtesy of Jennifer Sisson Photography

Once an officer, an individual is tossed into a culture with traditions passed orally through the generations—the annual St. Jude's Day Parade, the star, the uniform, the Blue Line one must quickly adopt. And each officer also begins to consider career aspirations—patrol life, leadership, detective, and office work, among others. Such hopes vary: retired officer John O'Shea never took an advancement test; his friend Joe DeLopez shot up the ranks and landed on the doorstep of the superintendent's post. Yet what officers maintain as necessary stands the command of an aspiration. The desire to do something, the pursuit of a career path, contend many officers, provides a worthwhile connection to the world of dreamers and idealists, a necessary relationship to serve those on the other side of the yellow police tape.

"We all want something," says O'Shea, "and while we might not all want the same thing, we at least have that desire in common, a hope for something in our lives. It's part of our police culture, but it's also part of our human culture. Having hopes connects us to our partner, our sergeant, but also to Joe on the street. At the minimum, we can all connect on that."

The Blue Line and the Red Tape

Despite its targeting by officers frustrated with the bureaucracy of the work as well as citizens wondering if their tax dollars might be better spent elsewhere, the Chicago Police Department has nevertheless evolved into a commendable unit gaining global recognition, a fact acknowledged by former Chicago Police officer Art Hannus, now the successful head of a private security firm, when he leans in and offers, "You know, there's a thing or two some Fortune 500 companies can learn from the Chicago Police Department; multimillion-dollar companies that are not nearly as efficient as the Chicago Police." Though, it should also be added, the Chicago Police Department remains an organization trailing behind in the modern-day communication methods of e-mail and voice mail. Detectives often snicker when an inquiring caller asks to leave a voice mail message. C.K. Rojas, who left his post as an officer in New Bern, North Carolina, to join the CPD, envisioned heading to a department advanced in all the latest weaponry and technology only to discover that Chicago remained rather archaic in some of its methods.

Despite the department's flaws, many officers relish the far-reaching

➤ *The Chicago Police Education and Training Academy currently resides in the city's West Loop neighborhood. The James J. Riordan Police Headquarters Building honors the life and career of a fallen Chicago officer James Riordan, who rose through the department's ranks until reaching the office of first deputy superintendent.*
Courtesy of Daniel P. Smith

scope of the CPD; among them is Detective John Folino. In the academy, Folino encountered a list of all the units, special patrols, and divisions of the Chicago Police Department—nearly 100 strong, to serve any situation and personality that may hit an international city inhabited by some 2.9 million residents.

"That's what's always surprised me," says Folino, "just how complex it all is and all the opportunities available. You want to be on the street? Fine. Want to be involved in the science aspect of police work? Got it. Legal? PR? Teach in the Academy? There's something for everyone."

But they all start at the same place—the Chicago Police Academy at Jackson and Throop. There, officers undergo the transformation to police life and culture. Recruits get pushed through classroom, physical, and scenario exercises to prepare for life as a Chicago officer.

"Everything in the academy is taught textbook, which is to say, the safest possible way," says officer Bob Rawa, a former instructor in the academy, "And everything that's taught there is based on incidents gone wrong." (Such training, which many officers discard as unrealistic in live street

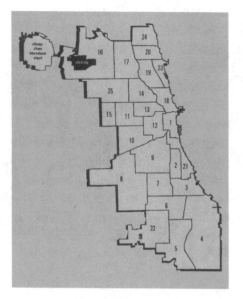

> *Map of Chicago Police Districts*

**AREA 1: DISTRICTS
2, 7, 8, 9, AND 21**

**AREA 2: DISTRICTS
3, 4, 5, 6, AND 22**

**AREA 3: DISTRICTS
18, 19, 20, 23, AND 24**

**AREA 4: DISTRICTS
1, 10, 11, 12, AND 13**

**AREA 5: DISTRICTS
14, 15, 16, 17, AND 25**

situations, serves to insulate the city hierarchy from liability—a "CYA" for top city officials. "Then they can always fall back on the fact that the officer didn't act as trained if something goes wrong," says one veteran officer.)

After graduation from the academy, officers take assignment to a district for one year as a probationary patrol officer. Some officers cringe at being assigned to the 16th District, a relatively quiet neighborhood on the Northwest Side that houses many city workers and working-class personnel, seeking instead the furious pace of a high-action district such as the 11th or 15th on the city's West Side. Other cadets, meanwhile, want nothing more than a modest introduction into urban police work, hoping their order reads District 012, which includes the Mexican-dominated Pilsen area, Taylor Street, and the gentrified West Loop, or District 013, the Near West Side district running just south of Humboldt Park to the Henry Horner public housing projects, districts that offer enough daily crime and personality to keep a cop busy without the consistent threat of whizzing bullets. Outside those with a little clout to toss around, most recruits have little say in their designation upon police academy graduation and take their assignment with a smirk or grudge but little outward complaint.

Each of the city's 25 police districts, a title long ago adopted over the New York–style precinct label, consists of gang and tactical teams, a community policing office, as well as three patrol units further divided into beats, between nine and 15, that represent subsections of a given district. On the top of Chicago Police patrol cars, a removable plate identifies the unit and beat of a given car—the last two numbers signaling the beat with the preceding numbers naming the district (#1522, for instance, would be 15th District, Beat 22). Since 1992, five Area Headquarters, wherein detectives are housed, have managed five districts each.

As officers move forward in their careers, some focus on a specialized city unit or advancement in rank, though hopes are not always realized. Opportunities in the department, as the aforementioned Folino discovered, are varied and unique. Some of the department's most heralded, active, and innovative units include:

- The CPD's **Detective Division**, once characterized in the 1960s television show *Crime Story,* carries a long history among the world's most storied law enforcement corps. Divided into five areas

> ➤ *A plaque in tribute to Officer James J. Riordan at the Chicago Police Academy honors the life and career of a fallen Chicago officer.*
> Courtesy of Daniel P. Smith

that each cover activity in five districts, detectives are assigned to one of three units: homicide/gangs/sex crimes; robbery/burglary/theft; and special victims. While many identify a detective's post as the department's premier assignment, others resist the meticulous nature of the work and its distance from the street.

- The department's **Organized Crime Division** focuses its efforts on large-scale illegal activities. Though frequently paired with federal and state task forces, the division handles the bulk of its work alone among its various units. The **Narcotics** and **Gang Intelligence Unit** addresses illegal narcotics operations through both street-level enforcement and lengthy criminal investigations. The **Gang Intelligence Section** identifies gang organizations involved in criminal activity and dispenses such information throughout the department. The **Vice Enforcement Unit** is charged with overseeing the detection and squelching

➤ *The Chicago Police Department's Detective Bureau has enjoyed repute as one of the nation's finest law enforcement divisions. On July 12, 1912, Chicago detectives gathered at 179 N. LaSalle for a bureau photograph. The first Chicago detectives constituted the department's best and brightest officers.*

Courtesy of the Chicago Public Library, Special Collections and Preservation Division

of criminal activities other than narcotics, including such Chicago staples as prostitution and gambling.

- Popularized by today's many television programs depicting their work, the **Forensic Services Section** offers scientific and technical expertise for the collection and analysis of evidence as well as crime reconstruction. The section includes a number of teams, specializing in specific evidence areas—photography, firearms, evidence evaluation, polygraph, and laser.
- The **Special Investigations CCAC Unit** investigates cases involving sexual abuse and assault of children under 13 as well as family- and institution-related cases of children under 18 (sex-crimes detectives handle most other sexually charged cases). Teaming with medical, psychological, and social service professionals, the CCAC takes on work that many cops seek to avoid. As one sex-crimes detective put it, "There's no way I could handle seeing this type of stuff with kids. No way."
- **Special Operations (SOS)** provides a ready, citywide unit responding to emergency situations and criminal hot spots. Among others, it includes the department's **SWAT** team, handling hostage, barricade, and terrorist events, as well as the canine program and marine/helicopter unit.
- Similar to SOS in its response to high-crime city areas, the **Targeted Response Unit** saturates areas to reinforce the efforts of district officers consumed by drug, gun, and gang problems. Under the direction of then-Superintendent Phil Cline, these units have been heralded for their role in reducing crime in volatile areas throughout the city.
- The **School Visitation Section** coordinates youth instructional and outreach programs such as GREAT and DARE as well as the Officer Friendly Program in elementary schools. Retired patrolman Willie Calabrese, the longtime Officer Friendly in the West Side's Austin neighborhood, was so distinguished in the neighborhood that some witnesses and suspects refused to speak to anyone in the district except Uncle Willie.
- Initiated by the reform-minded administration of Orlando Wilson though recommended as early as 1932, the **Internal Affairs Division (IAD)**, composed of sworn officers, oversees disciplinary

matters involving alleged or suspected violations by Chicago officers. IAD joins with the **Office of Professional Standards (OPS)**, staffed by civilian investigators and founded in 1974, in being the department's chief units handling officer misconduct. In 2004, the units collectively handled 5,555 investigations of officers, 770 of which had findings sustained.[7] Some officers view the IAD office, in particular, with contempt, showing the sustaining power of the Blue Line. One former officer reports that after moving to a post in IAD, his best friend, a fellow Chicago cop, refused to speak with him for months.

And while the organization of the department, its many layers demanding different strengths and rejecting specific weaknesses, contributes to the culture of the Chicago Police, it nevertheless falls short of capturing the true breadth of a department cloaked in tradition yet adding new characters and chapters each day. Any description of the department's flow chart fails to capture the color and essence of the Chicago Police culture, a society of star-wearing cops inside the yellow police line and charging through every floor of the high-rise, which includes retired lieutenant Cindy Pontoriero, who became the first female detective in the department's history and counts those days among her most memorable; Rick King, a former officer in the now defunct Felony Decoy Unit, which had him playing a priest to catch sinners; retired officer George Salituro, who found his place among the airplanes and witnessed O'Hare International Airport's evolution from the open prairie northwest of the city into an international destination; the late Bob Rawa, who found his place in the department among the dogs; and newly minted detective John Folino Jr., a fast-rising officer matching an MBA with muscle. Such individuals have capitalized on the inherent opportunity in the department and demonstrate the scope of its organization. Their stories also place us in a culture that distinguishes the police life from the civilian life—their life from ours.

ALL I EVER WANTED TO BE: RETIRED LIEUTENANT CINDY PONTORIERO

★

Cindy Pontoriero recalls the old days with a warm spirit and enthusiastic laughter.

"Three tests, do you believe it?" she asks. "They had the police matron's exam, the policewoman's exam, and the patrolman's exam. They just didn't know what to do with us women," she quips, one of the many times she activates her tell-it-like-it-is ideology. It was a different world then, says Pontoriero. And after she took the policewoman's exam in 1965, the Chicago Police Academy beckoned in 1967.

She recalls: "The first class they called was 30 ladies, and then I was in the second class they put through the academy, with only 15 women," she says. "I was never one of the first-class, head-of-the-class types, so I had to wait a while."

The male cadets, segregated from the female cadets, were not to fraternize with the women, but Pontoriero fires a jab at that edict.

"I still met my husband in the academy, anyway," she says of her husband of 32 years, Kenny, a veteran Chicago cop who retired in 1993.

Upon leaving the academy, all female officers were assigned to the youth divisions, and away Pontoriero went to Area Four at Maxwell and Morgan streets, a now-defunct Chicago station best known as the façade for the television show Hill Street Blues. *Wearing a skirt and pumps patterned after airline uniforms, Pontoriero did what she calls "the ma thing"—dealing with missing children, abandoned or neglected youth, and processing juvenile crime.*

"You ended up doing all the same things as the youth officers, except they worked in plainclothes and got paid more money," she says.

Pontoriero recalls the many crusades she embarked on in those youth division days. She shares the stories in her uncompromising voice as if the extra effort she pushed was a requirement of the job.

"Everything you do is an experience," she says, "and I realized that I could have an impact. You'd get kids out of these horrible conditions and you'd spend your own money to get them food or clothes. Of course, I could do this because at the time I didn't have a family of my own; I could get personally involved."

Give her time, however, and she'll release another robust laugh and return to thoughts of those damn uniforms.

"You know, they'd send you to the West Side and you'd want to say, 'What the hell am I supposed to do in this costume?'

"But I always hiked up the skirt a little and I always carried my .38 with me. You gotta have at least a .38 with you or you might as well not have anything at all."

————————————————★————————————————

She flashes a picture of a 1980 holiday party and pride fills her face.

The staged photograph shows a gathering of detectives from Chicago's Area Five, all with dizzying grins and shimmering eyes. For 63-year-old Cindy Pontoriero, looking at this photo sparks a smile and sigh, and a craving to do it all over again.

"That's me. I was a pretty one, wasn't I?" says Pontoriero, pointing to a rosy-cheeked, thirtysomething female amid the glossy faces of nearly 40 male colleagues. In the photo, Pontoriero, the lone woman, wears short hair, a heavy turtleneck sweater, and a knee-length skirt that meets leather boots.

"They were all more like brothers to me," she says of her former detective colleagues. "They were a great bunch and I was lucky to have all of them."

Pausing for a moment, she scratches under her right eye and gazes at the photo a final time before moving ahead to others. "It broke my heart that I could never go back to the detective division," she says of her final 14 police years spent in the patrol division and away from her beloved detective's role. "Maybe I didn't knock on the right doors or maybe I stopped making myself visible, but it just broke my heart."

The passion formed early for Cindy Pontoriero. She never knew any cops or detectives save the few who passed in front of her on Chicago's streets.

"In those days," she says, "women weren't the police and they certainly weren't dicks."

The passage of time coupled with aggressive wits, however, would change all of that.

In 1961 at the age of 19, Cindy Pontoriero became a civilian employee with the Chicago Police Department, a stenographer in the department's old Shakespeare District on the near Northwest Side. She took notes and typed up reports, all at a single desk on the station's third floor surrounded by the movement of the district's detectives. In time, she became fascinated with the process of police work.

"From then on," she says, "being a detective was all I ever wanted in life. Just that. I was in awe of the whole thing—the work they did. Nobody had rights then. There were bondsmen and lawyers in the station. Guys sitting around until they confessed. The stories, the people around me. The natural progression of things was that I would want to be one of these."

But in the 1960s, women played only minor roles in the department. In 1967, Pontoriero entered the Chicago Police Academy, a member of Chicago's second group of female officers, and accepted her assignment to the West Side's Area Four Youth Division, the de facto appointment for all sworn female officers. She carried her .38 along with her department-issued purse and took aggressively to her job. "I would haunt people and, I tell you, I have a big mouth and I used it."

Still, Pontoriero's thoughts never strayed far from her most ardent desire to be a detective. Women did not carry the detective's star, but that didn't stop Pontoriero from imagining it.

"The key was to keep making yourself visible because you could get detailed out," says Pontoriero. "You had to let people know you were there. That's the only way, as a woman, you'd even have a prayer."

In November 1970, Pontoriero earned a temporary assignment to the First District as part of its Operation Holiday initiative, giving her a break from her Youth Division duties. By positioning themselves among holiday shoppers eager to spend their money and thieves eager to take it before it was spent, Pontoriero, along with three other female officers, proved their mettle and insisted to the district's commander that they could provide a valuable service.

"I always wanted to do more than they wanted me to do," says Pontoriero today as she settles into her recollection. "We had been involved with the tact teams and I told the commander that we could do decoy missions. I told him, 'If they see two guys riding around in a car, they're gonna know it's the police. But if they see a man and woman, they won't think twice.' I just saw the possibilities and tried to get him to see them, too."

Pontoriero's persuasive powers paid off as she and another female officer remained on the district's tact team, working nights. While there, the detective's exam neared and Pontoriero seized the brief opportunity before her.

"All the guys I worked with signed up for the test and since that was what I always wanted to be I signed up, too," she says.

Despite the fact that women could not take the detective's exam, Pontoriero worked around the issue with some clever paperwork, writing her name as C.L. Pontoriero and her district as 001 on the exam application, foregoing both her first name as well as her permanent assignment to Area 4's Youth Division. Neither caught the attention of department staff.

"I knew once they stamped my application, they couldn't take it back," she admits.

While waiting to take the exam, one later opened to other women, Pontoriero prepared diligently. She attended law classes as well as taking a course at the University of Illinois called "Fundamentals of Criminal Investigation." She filled her free time studying for the exam.

"I utilized every asset I had because I was single and I could make it my life's sole mission at the time. I wasn't concerned with the bigger picture. I didn't think beyond. It was take the test and pass it."

In June 1972, Pontoriero realized the dream she had set for herself nearly a dozen years earlier as a 19-year-old civilian employee, when she became Chicago's first sworn woman detective. Media attention then put Pontoriero in the limelight, a spot she detested because it placed her under the microscope.

> ➢ *Upon taking her assignment to the Area 4 Youth Division, Cindy Pontoriero, who would later become the city's first female detective, ventured to Morgan and Maxwell streets on the city's Near Southwest Side. The former Area 4 headquarters now houses the University of Illinois at Chicago Police, but is best known as the façade for the popular* Hill Street Blues *television program*
> Courtesy of Daniel P. Smith

"I said to people that the more notoriety I got, the more hostility I would get. All I wanted was acceptance, because without that I wouldn't be taught and I wouldn't learn. I wasn't more worthy of attention than anyone else," says Pontoriero. "My thought was never to pave the way for anybody else or to open doors. I never wanted to be a trailblazer; I just wanted to be a detective.

"Listen," she commands, "I was raised Italian and it's a patriarchal world. I wasn't a pushover, but I didn't care to compete with the men. I didn't care about challenging the status quo. I just wanted to be a detective and that was the end of the thought."

Though images from the 1920s and '30s picture female "detectives" in Chicago, Pontoriero was indeed the city's first woman to ever earn the detective rank upon taking and passing the detective's exam—nothing was ever handed to her.

"At the time, the detective's test was the only department test that was taken and scored right there. You walked out of that building and knew your score right there," tells Pontoriero. "It took the clout out of it."

As a detective in Area Five, a massive assignment covering the city's entire Northwest Side, Pontoriero encountered the career she envisioned long ago. The job, with its constant movement and criminal puzzles, did not disappoint.

"The be all and end all," she says with a grin. "Being a detective is one of the few jobs where you get the middle and the end. Very seldom as a cop do you get the rest of the story—and that's the best part." Pontoriero spent nearly 18 years as a detective in violent crimes, covering homicide and aggravated assault and emerging as a specialist in sex crimes. Rape and sex crimes, she says, became hot topics in the 1980s and led to the formation of separate North Side and South Side units to address such crimes. All female detectives in 1980, including Pontoriero, were sent to one of the sections. By 1981, with the closing of the short-lived sex crime units, Pontoriero returned to Area Five on the Northwest Side and her traditional role in violent crimes.

"I was never trying to be Annie Oakley; I didn't buy all that 'anything you can do I can do better' garbage. I wanted to be a complement, not competition, because that's really how things get solved—when everybody recognizes what they can do and what they can add to the process."

She tells of a young man who operated throughout the North Side, preying upon older women who visited cemeteries alone. He would rape and assault them, leaving them with lingering wounds. Pontoriero and other detectives would often play the role of decoys, dressing and playing the part, hoping to lure the criminal into action. Unsuccessful in those efforts, they happened upon a picture book of former penitentiary inmates. When they visited past victims, one lady picked her assailant from the book, and Chicago Police soon had the man in custody.

"I was in the area station that day when the victims came in one by one and identified him. He knew he lost right there," she says.

"The Gotcha," as Pontoriero calls it, always provided the climactic end, the aspect of detective work that most motivated her.

"To find the bad guy—not necessarily to physically get him, but to go through the steps to identify the criminal. That's the thrill of it all. Then, you follow it through to court. You put the case together so thoroughly and patiently that there are no holes. The reward is when you hear that word 'guilty.'"

Today, Pontoriero tells of lasting relationships with some victims, check-in calls to Pontoriero letting her know how life had progressed. Many Chicago detectives experience the same phenomenon, a sign that relationships blossom from their unusual set of circumstances.

"Long after the case was done," she says of those continuing relationships, which survived the crime, the pursuit, and the process of justice. "Yeah, you got the bad guy, but you also gave closure to people so that they could go to bed at night."

Now, at age 63, Pontoriero is no less passionate about detective work, no less enthusiastic about the career she landed upon. She sits in her kitchen, wearing a sweatshirt that proclaims in rainbow embroidery, "Somebody special calls me Grandma." Her energy level high, Pontoriero rarely gives her lungs the opportunity for recovery. A Chicago Police scanner sounds in the background while a glass casing of her four police stars hangs on a hallway wall. Her husband Kenny, a 69-year-old retired West Side copper, arrives home from a part-time security job and she shouts at him: "Hey, Kenny, is there anything you want to say about me being a copper?"

Kenny, known as Iggy through his cop days, takes stock of the question. A former Taylor Street Italian kid with hefty shoulders and stinging wit, he moves to the dining room table and sits. He focuses his eyes ahead and says: "Yeah, I got something to say. That she did her job well." He then nods his head over and over, confident those words provide all that is necessary.

Still upon the table rests the reminder of that holiday party 25 years ago and it catches Pontoriero's glance once again. Peering down at the photograph, she flashes a smile, one equally magnificent as the one she shines in the photo. She retells the old line, the one repeated by so many old-timers, the one about missing the clowns but not the circus.

"But I miss 'em both," she says. "I miss them both terribly—the clowns and the circus. I took the civilian job with the police because it was a job. Now, I'm just so grateful I got to be the police. It was the best life I ever could've asked for."

She continues to stare at the photo, a smile on her face.

"It was all a special time," she says. "A real special time."

INVITING CRIME:
OFFICER RICK KING

───────────────────────★───────────────────────

It was never in Rick King's life plan to be a cop. Even today, King admits, "It was a complete fluke."

As a senior business administration major at Governors State University in Chicago's south suburbs, King took an elective course that offered credit for taking the Chicago Police Department exam and two suburban police tests. His grade was based on a paper discussing each of the exams and a cumulative paper at semester's end that compared and contrasted each exam.

"Four papers and no classes to attend—I thought it seemed easy enough," he says. "This was at a time in the mid-1970s when the hiring practices of the CPD were being challenged left and right."

In 1975, King joined 24,000 others in taking the Chicago Police test at Lane Technical High School on the city's North Side. He then took police tests in the southwestern suburbs of Evergreen Park and Alsip. He wrote his papers, got his grade, received his diploma, and started work as an electrician, the idea of a career with the Chicago Police Department no more than a distant thought in his mind. He began working for a private electrical contractor and settled into his new job.

"But then the boss came by and said he was taking off to Aruba for all of January and we wouldn't be working the entire month," King recalls. "All of a sudden, I was an out-of-work electrician."

But as luck would have it, a letter sat in King's mailbox when he arrived home that same day. The letter said that if he wanted to be a Chicago Police cadet, he should report to the academy on January 3, 1977. And so Rick King joined the Chicago Police Department because, above any other consideration, he needed a job.

"I didn't have any relatives on the job. You'll hear of

*some others who will tell you that being a Chicago cop was
all they ever wanted to be—like it's written in the stars.
That wasn't me," he says. "I was unemployed and they
offered me a job."*

*By the summer of 1977, Rick King moved from cadet
to patrol officer, something he never thought he'd be.*

*Within a few years, King would be something else he
never envisioned: a priest.*

———————————————★———————————————

Over a million people jammed Chicago's Grant Park on the evening of
July 3, 2005. The city's 28th annual fireworks display would soon take center
stage, triggering oohs and aahs to spill from the mouths of young and old.
From all walks of life and all corners of the Chicago area—and around the
Midwest—the parade of faces moved in front of Rick King as he sat in a parked
police squad car on State Street facing north onto Lake Street. Just in case,
King called it. Just in case something went down. He was a presence, a sign
that the Chicago Police would be around to stifle any potential problems.

But there was a time when Rick King wasn't there just in case. A time
not so long ago when he tracked each face that entered the park. A time
when he could pick from the crowd the ones he'd have to watch, a tingle of
instinct signaling the ones he'd likely see again later in the night.

"You'd look at people and say, 'He's a pickpocket.' You'd watch everybody
and you'd look for the thieves," says King, a hearty man with strawberry
blond hair and a pair of glasses that fill his round, friendly face. "It becomes
a sixth sense you develop, just like some of the real good coppers who just
know—the guys who say, 'He's got a gun' or 'That's a stolen car.' And you
know what? They're usually right."

And while a small part of King misses that attention to duty, another
part is glad to see that disruption gone, the cynicism laid to rest, and his
watchful eye toned down.

"I'd be out at a sporting event with my kids and I'd have my eyes on
everybody—on my own time," King says. "And then my kids would want
to go to the Taste of Chicago or downtown for a parade. I'd be caught down
there all day with work and I wouldn't want to go in my personal life. It's not
the best way to live. You know what's out there and so you're looking for it.

It didn't matter if I was on or off duty. I made hundreds of off-duty arrests because pickpocket thefts are always happening in Chicago. It was my job and I knew I was doing a good thing. Still, I didn't like always being on edge."

King spent over 10 years in the Chicago Police Department's Felony Decoy Unit, a specialized and covert unit wanting crime to happen; in fact, King and his colleagues sought to be the victims themselves. The group would encounter a crime pattern and then set up a similar scenario, inviting the criminals to emerge from the city's landscape and commit their acts of wrongdoing. In short, the unit's objective stood to catch criminals in the midst of their crimes, luring them to commit their acts in clear sight. The urban cop's bait-and-hook show.

"It wasn't an easy thing to decoy felons," King says. "It was a challenge because it's not something you can make up or just create. The person has to commit the felony on you.

"I don't think I ever had one civilian come and testify in all my years with the Decoy Unit. The victim had gotten their wallet back and wasn't about to waste time testifying against the guy in court. If we could get the thief with a decoy, then we knew we'd be in court the next day. We knew the case wouldn't be tossed."

In teams of three or four, King and his partners would go out, each watching the other's back and seeking to bring crime directly into their lives. A rash of robberies occurring on nurses as they left Cook County Hospital and walked to the El station prompted action from King's group. His female partner, dressed in nurse's garb, left the hospital's doors and walked to the train with her purse in clear sight. Seeing an easy, naive target, the robbers would strike, feeling assured of an easy theft.

"What you wanted to show the robbers is that you wouldn't be trouble for them," says King. "Make yourself an easy target and they'd hit."

As sure as anyone could predict the sun's rising each morning, the robber would strike, and King, covertly standing on the street or El platform dressed as a priest, would apprehend the robber as he attempted to snatch the purse.

"One of us guys would be doing close cover. Just blending in behind the scenes to keep our decoy protected," says King. "And then you play the game of ascending dominance. And it's all worth it when you throw the cuffs on the criminal.

"You'd begin to wonder, then, that if this guy victimized the police, how many citizens has he taken from without getting caught?"

King, now a 53-year-old canine officer with 28 years on the job and a son, Ryan, following his footsteps, recalls his decade of work in the Felony Decoy Unit (a now defunct unit that morphed into what is presently the Mass Transit Tact Team) as a time of humor, good deeds, and autonomy.

"It wasn't a unit you requested to go to; you were chosen," he remembers. "They asked a lot from you, but they took care of you, too. You had a lot of freedom because it was one of the few units in the city with covert status. All you had to do was a 'pull' every two hours—just a call in to say that you were okay. You could have a beard, long hair, and carry any weapon. You were supposed to blend in to the city."

While his time these days is spent in the department's Canine Unit with Deny, a healthy shepherd who once recovered 320 kilos of cocaine, it is his time with the Felony Decoy Unit that is at the heart of his Chicago Police career.

"It was a great place to be when you were a young cop," says King, adding, "you know, when you're still full of piss and vinegar."

Often in his role as a priest blending into the city's background, King provided close cover to any number of his colleagues who played the role of would-be victim, the easy target inviting crime to come his or her way.

"I'll never forget Art Novitt and his Superman costume," says King, recalling one of the unit's most notorious tales. "His wife was an excellent seamstress and put together this Superman costume for him that would have made Hollywood jealous. Fit him perfectly."

Novitt served as the centerpiece in a pickpocket set-up in the city's underground El stations. The group positioned Novitt, clad in the royal blue outfit with a blaring *S* on the chest, in one of the worker's booths. The team then removed the hinges of the door and rigged fire extinguishers to release cloudy gas upon the door being pushed open by Novitt. The act only began, however, when the decoy, playing the part of a drunken construction worker with money hanging out of his pocket, was the robbery target.

"So the decoy was lying on the bench," tells King, "and we'd see the guy come by with big eyes once he spotted the money. And when he went for the money, Novitt would push open the door, smoke would come up, and you'd hear Novitt say, 'Halt, wrongdoer.'"

King and other team members then emerged from beyond the subway's corners to discover Novitt and a stunned thief amid the cloud of gas.

"We'd say 'Superman, Superman, what's the problem?' and he'd say how this guy was trying to take the man's wallet. We'd thank Superman and lead the man away. Then, Novitt ran down the platform and it would look like he jumped off the side and began flying down the tunnel. You couldn't help but chuckle at the situation."

The next day in court the thief pleaded guilty, something King says all the pickpockets did, given that the frequent consequence—30 days' probation and time served—offered little punishment. In the courtroom, however, the judge asked the defendant if he had anything to offer in defense. And this rare time, the defendant spoke.

As King retells it, calling upon his repertoire of voices to play the role of judge and thief: "The guy says, 'Well, yes, your honor, I would like to say something. It is true, I did take the man's wallet, but it wasn't the cops who arrested me, your honor. It was Superman.' All I remember was the judge shaking his head, thinking this one was new, and then giving the guy 30 days and evaluation by a doctor.

"You have to allow yourself a laugh or two on this job, you have to break the monotony of things because most of what you see is the negative—it's 'gallows humor,' making light of awful situations just to save your own sanity."

➤ *A mural inside police headquarters at 35th and Michigan represents a typical Chicago neighborhood scene.*

Courtesy of Jennifer Sisson Photography

In the Felony Decoy Unit, King and his cohorts frequently turned to pickpockets because, as King chirps, "There's never a shortage of those in Chicago. Whenever there were no specific patterns to investigate, you went for the pickpockets."

And some of those pickpockets, recalls King, were downright masterful. "If you didn't know what you were looking for, you'd never know. Some of them were that skilled and that smooth," he says.

For example, there were the Dinglebells, a group of Colombian men who would enter Chicago during some of the city's prime events—the Taste of Chicago, the Christmas shopping season—and have a profitable day of wallet theft. The Dinglebells were so adept at thievery, something they did around the world, because they trained their pickpockets with electronic bells. In training, they had to remove a wallet from a purse and not allow the wallet's sensor to come in contact with a sensor in their shirt pocket. If the sensors connected, then the bell sounded. The rigorous training allowed the group to earn global notoriety for their illegal yet impressive criminal skill.

"These were the guys you really wanted; they were the ones who could really hurt you," says King. "They could pull ten thefts a day without a problem. And that would impact your crime stats and make it look like you were failing. You had to look at these guys from above, get an overhead view with some guys on the ground; that's the only way you were going to beat them."

Upon leaving the Felony Decoy Unit for the Canine Unit in 1987, King immediately felt a sense of loss.

"When you do something for so long, it's difficult to change gears," he says. But now, nearly 20 years after his last decoy situation, King sees his time in the Felony Decoy Unit in a different light.

"I thought maybe I was pushing my luck. I was shot in the leg, stabbed in the knee and arm, so there did come a time to leave," he says. "But most of the memories are good ones, and I don't have regrets. You're the person called in to solve the problem and there's value in that work."

King pauses, taking in the crowds that head to the city's summer fireworks display. He looks back at Deny, the shepherd peering out the back driver's side window, and then returns his own eyes to the street.

"Yeah," he admits, "a part of me would love to play the priest again, especially on a day like today—some of the real smooth pickpockets are out tonight."

THE MAYOR OF O'HARE: RETIRED OFFICER GEORGE SALITURO

———————————————★———————————————

On a sunny but cool April morning, George Salituro drives around Chicago's O'Hare International Airport with the window down and a cigarette dangling from his left hand. With confidence and ease, he navigates through lanes of traffic, simultaneously lifting his cigarette to signal points of interest. Each gesture precedes a personal footnote—a brief oral history report from Salituro about what once was, what now is, or what someday may be.

To outsiders and perhaps even Chicagoans themselves, Chicago's O'Hare Airport might as well be a maze with a reward at the end—a chaotic movement of structures and streets that is a city all its own. But Sal, as most everyone calls him, knows O'Hare well. He has grown up around the airport. To be certain, O'Hare is Sal's place.

He points to the Hilton Hotel.

"That wasn't there when I started."

He points to a multi-level parking structure.

"Now that," he says, "was a parking lot, but it was just the one level, just the street level. And back then you could even park on the street for a couple minutes. Nobody would bother you."

At today's O'Hare, one existing in the post–September 11 world, police squads and parking personnel advise people to move along. Sitting cars today mean something different than they did to Sal 30 years ago. "You know, there wasn't even a fence here," he says signaling to the half-mile-long stretch of eight-foot-high fence crowned with barbed wire.

Later, he points north.

"And God knows what they have planned for up north. But that's the way the airport's moving these days," says Sal. While uncertainty guides his voice, so too does pride that things have come this far, that O'Hare is still growing and

changing—a work in progress.

Of course, he remembers the early days of the infancy of O'Hare Airport and its simplistic grandeur. Now one of the world's busiest airports, O'Hare emerged from the empty fields immediately northwest of the city to become a bustling community, a space hosting approximately 200,000 visitors daily. For most of that history, Sal was there, his silver Chicago Police Department star a polished symbol of his duty.

As he continues to speak of O'Hare, its history, and its people, his words are sincere and unruffled. Like a father recalling the exploits of a son, he pauses frequently to look up and hash through some details in his own mind so as not to misrepresent O'Hare's story.

In a way, O'Hare is almost like another son.

"Yeah," chuckles Sal. "I sometimes think that's not too far off."

———————————————————★———————————————————

While planes flew overhead, George Salituro was contemplating his next pitch. A player/coach on one of the league's top teams, Sal let the 16-inch softball glide from his hand toward the plate.

The O'Hare Airport softball league was serious business—to Sal, his Chicago Police teammates, and all the other two-dozen teams in the league, a compilation of workers from airlines and airport hotels. Everybody in those days had a team, and most people knew one another and their softball talents. That was O'Hare in the late 1960s and 1970s. "Hellos" and "See ya' laters" and "Good games" blanketing much of the airport jargon. Today's O'Hare is a different story. Less fraternizing and, sad to say, no more 16-inch.

But in the 1970s, there wasn't only a softball league on O'Hare's grounds with formal teams and uniforms, but the Department of Aviation actually donated the land for fields. Not only did airlines and hotels field teams, but so too did the Chicago Police Department's O'Hare unit, a frequent league champion. Imagine the response today if somebody asked where the police presence was at O'Hare and another person in the know responded, "They're playing the championship softball game out back."

> ➤ *In the midst of the 1967 snowstorm, Sal (center with bottle) and a host of stranded passengers found revelry and good laughs in an airport lounge.*
Courtesy of George Salituro

But that was Sal's O'Hare in those days, as magnificent a world as he ever encountered.

"Socializing and window cleaning," says Sal, the latter referring to the police department's public relations priority at the young airport.

Take the blizzard of 1967. With over 22 inches of snow blanketing the ground, O'Hare Airport was in lock-down. No one in. No one out. So what were airline workers, stranded passengers, and Chicago's airport cops to do but transform an airport lounge into a functional nightclub.

"The sergeant over here," recalls Sal, "got a call from somebody telling them that things were getting a little loud in the lounge, so the sergeant said, 'Don't worry, I'll send Sal over there to calm things down.' The guy said, 'Sal? He's in the middle of it all.'

"But those were the times then. You hear people talking about the good ol' days and that was them."

Sal, who in his early adult years had contemplated a vocation with the Servite Order and its missionary work, never had any aspirations to join the police department, nor did any idealistic thinking compel him to pursue work with the Chicago Police.

"In those days," he says, recalling the late 1950s and early 1960s, "you went to the gas, electric, police, or fire just to have a job."

His Chicago Police career began in 1961, and his assignment to O'Hare followed one year later, just as O'Hare gained the title of "world's busiest airport." He recalls the late Mayor Richard J. Daley referring to O'Hare as "the threshold to the City of Chicago" and expressing his desire to have a tidy and professional police presence at the airport to make Chicago's guests welcomed and impressed.

"There were a lot of young guys at the beginning because the city wanted to create a good image. And it took a special guy to be assigned here. He had to be compassionate. He had to like people and want to help them and be willing to go out of his way to do so.

"At the beginning, it was young guys who came out here and stayed; now, it's guys in the twilight of their careers. The younger guys want action, but this is where a lot of your old-timers want to be," he says, noting the seniority process that now governs O'Hare appointments.

Sal says the early years of O'Hare were less about solving crime and more about friendly, kind work with socializing at the core; he even met his wife, who worked for American Airlines, in the airport's chapel.

"You know it was basically just helping people out. Telling them where this was or that was," he says. "There weren't many police problems— maybe an occasional body in the parking lot. But it was all about socializing out here, all about making friends."

Although he had opportunities to leave and did one yearlong stint investigating crimes against senior citizens, Sal spent 32 of his 34 years in the department at O'Hare.

"It was too nice out here; I never wanted to return to the district," says Sal, a puff of smoke following the comment. "It was never like going to work."

Today, moments after navigating his way through a complex series of underground tunnels, Sal stands in the airport's round building, at what he calls "State and Madison"—the center of O'Hare's physical universe. With a Chicago Police Department baseball cap covering his head and thick glasses resting on his slender nose, he begins a stroll through the airport's terminals. Like a tour guide, he shares facts and anecdotes, stopping to chat with old friends along the way. There are few with whom he does not exchange a smile or nod of the head, perhaps something that has been conditioned in his demeanor.

"It's second nature to walk around these days," he says, taking a quick left turn and continuing into another terminal. "The Chicago officers here today are always walking around outside of security because that's their primary duty now. Just a handful of guys walk around in plain clothes on the inside."

Since September 11, the airport has become a more serious, intense place. It's not quite like it used to be, he says, "but I could survive it. I'd just go around making friends." Yet, he recalls past moments in which the easygoing nature of his assignment at O'Hare was challenged.

"American Airlines Flight 191 crashed on the north end of the field," he says of the 1979 crash that once held the title as the nation's deadliest commercial airline disaster. "The engine fell off and they lost over 250 people."

Earlier that decade, coming in on a foggy, snowy night in 1972, a North Central Airlines plane missed the runway on its landing and crashed into a nearby hanger.

"Right after it happens, you're there to preserve the scene, you're there to do work," he says before halting his speech, directing his eyes

➤ *In the pre-9/11 days, O'Hare Airport, says Sal (seen here on the pitcher's mound), was a haven of good times and socializing. A softball league comprised of teams from airlines, airport hotels, and the Chicago Police Department's O'Hare unit tells of days long past.*

Courtesy of George Salituro

to the ground for a moment. "Trying to find all the body parts. Those were the times I didn't so much like it out here."

He shares the story of a hijacker holding up a Northwest flight on the ground, causing commotion and concern to run rampant throughout the airport.

"As the guy released everybody," says Sal, "he tried to get off with all the others by shaving his beard. But we weren't having it."

He ceases his walk for a brief chat with a former colleague, exchanging a modest laugh before resuming his forward movement. Steps later, a call of "Hey, Sal" rises from over his shoulder and he turns to see a female officer waving. He replies with his typical greeting—a wave of the hand, a tip of his hat.

"I miss this place when it was smaller," he says. "You could have a lot of close relationships with people."

He begins speaking of O'Hare's biggest challenge to police work during his three-decade tenure—the extension of the city's Blue Line train to the airport in 1984, a move lauded by many city folk as it allowed would-be travelers the ease of public transportation, yet detested by many law enforcement staff for its ease in inviting the criminal element to the airport.

"When they brought the CTA out here," he says, "it became easier for the worker and traveler to get here, but also for the bums and thieves."

Petty thievery proved the predominant crime as the O'Hare unit averaged 700 arrests a month, says Sal. The work existed in sharp contrast to the good-humored and friendly atmosphere once so dominant.

"For a while it was exciting and interesting, but after a while it became old hat. It was the same guys over and over. It lasted for about three or four years and then the Department of Aviation got an ordinance passed that only ticketed passengers and employees were allowed in the terminals."

One of the homeless men who made O'Hare a temporary shelter was Bill Hampton, notable only for his sibling relationship to Fred Hampton, the notorious head of Chicago's Black Panther party. Hampton collected luggage carts from passengers and returned them, keeping the quarter the cart cost to rent. Upon retirement, Sal received a scribbled note from Hampton thanking Sal for always treating him with respect.

Sal slips the note forward, simply saying, "That there's a note I got from Bill Hampton when I retired. Nice fella."

➤ *Mayor Eugene Sawyer congratulates Sal for his 32-years of service at O'Hare Airport in a City Hall ceremony.*
Courtesy of George Salituro

Even today, Sal cannot escape O'Hare. Over a decade after retirement, he currently holds a part-time position with Host Marriott, one of the airport's major concessionaires, collecting money from drop safes and serving as a liaison to the Chicago Police.

"I've always felt a personal stake in this place, especially since I met my wife out here. I grew up with this place." He stops to observe the crowd of travelers. Grinning, he says, "It's funny, you know, that everybody comes and goes from this place so quick. They can't wait to leave. They hustle to their flight and can't wait to take off. And then me? I never really wanted to leave this place at all—it was just too good to me. I'm in no hurry at all."

SEND IN THE DOGS: OFFICER BOB RAWA

──────────────★──────────────

It's November 6, 2003. And it's Sando's last day on the job.

Only he doesn't know it.

He goes about his business as usual, supporting the only partner he's ever known. Nothing is different. He remains as diligent now as the day he began, as faithful now as ever, as committed to the team effort of Chicago Police work as a cop can be.

His partner, Bob Rawa, experiences mixed emotions. He knows it's Sando's last day and wishes he could tell him, communicate to him in some way what the last four years have meant. How Sando always stood by his side. How Sando found what others couldn't. What Sando has meant to the city. And to him.

Saying farewell to a partner is never simple, never clean, and Rawa acknowledges his difficulties.

But Sando's days of police work are behind him. He's retiring now. And it's back to civilian life—so to speak.

──────────────★──────────────

He'll never be able to look at a Teletubby the same way again.

In the summer of 2002, Chicago canine officer Bob Rawa responded to a call from 7th District officers to bring the dogs for a car search. There, in the parking lot of the Englewood police station on Chicago's South Side, Rawa and his German shepherd, Sando, played their usual roles: Rawa serving orders, Sando carrying forth the task, and Rawa interpreting Sando's actions.

But this day, Sando's attention was focused on a Teletubby nearby. Despite orders from Rawa to sniff elsewhere, the dog would not be diverted; his attention remained on the Teletubby.

"I was starting to get pretty pissed with [Sando], so I picked up the Teletubby and threw it to the ground . . . and he was right back on it," Rawa says.

One of the first things canine officers learn in the academy is to trust the dog's instincts, having faith that the animal can do things the officer cannot. "When you're training your dog, you have to establish trust—just as you would with any partner—and understand why that trust is necessary," says Rawa. "If he's telling you there's dope there, it's there. If he's growling, then somebody's around. Maybe you can't see him. Maybe you can't hear him. But you have to trust your dog."

Perhaps there was more to this Teletubby and Sando's fascination with it. Rawa picked up the Teletubby and noticed a zipper on the bottom. Unzipping it, he pulled out a white tube sock. As several rocks of crack cocaine dropped to the blacktop, Rawa was reminded of Sando's abilities.

"It sounds corny, but Sando gave me a look like, 'See, stupid,'" says Rawa. "That's the honest truth."

And so the journey goes for Rawa, a six-year officer in Chicago's Canine Unit, and his dogs, the retired Sando and his current Czechoslovakian Shepherd, King. Canine police officers serve as specialists in a city that looks to exhaust all avenues to solve crime. Chicago employs 37 canine street handlers, primarily to search for narcotics and criminals, in addition to 18 officers who work with bomb dogs. The human-dog tandems constitute an exclusive unit with unique skills adding to the city's efforts.

Yet, in a profession where human partners are the norm, Rawa, 39, a 16-year veteran of the Chicago Police Department, has chosen his own path—with Sando and King as his partners and the citywide Canine Unit as his mission.

"He is my partner," Rawa says of King now, following Sando's retirement in 2003 due to hip problems. "I haven't worked with another copper for years, and that's fine with me. Here, I have a partner who doesn't care where and when we eat or where we go. All he cares about is being let out every once in a while to take care of business. The work is play to him."

Rawa estimates that 85 percent of his work with the Canine Unit involves narcotics searches. He says people will hide drugs anywhere—from Teletubbies to a car's gas tank—carriers hollow out the tank to half of its capacity in order to store drugs.

"The police can turn a car like that upside down and find nothing. The dogs can find the drugs and find them quick," he says.

➤ *Canine officer Bob Rawa poses with Sando, his German shepherd partner of nearly five years. Rawa says of the citywide Canine Unit: "The whole city is our oyster."*
Courtesy of Bob Rawa

Some of the scores yield impressive results. Rawa once discovered over 800 pounds of marijuana and several firearms in the nine-foot wall of a West Side home with Sando, perhaps his former dog's most notable accomplishment.

"We got word from an informant that the guy had it hidden in a wall and that's all we knew. We were there searching and searching until I noticed a wall with no electrical outlet or light switch; that sparked my interest. I sent Sando at it and he was all over it," says Rawa. "That's when this job's best—when you're beating the bad guys at their own game."

And Rawa appreciates his role in the team effort, the specialized work he and his dog bring to complement the officers who have worked their own angles before calling upon the Canine Unit's skills.

"I've always enjoyed the feeling of the dog finding something where I can then go tell another officer, 'Here's what you're after.' There's a lot of satisfaction in that. You're contributing to the team cause."

After receiving a business degree from St. Xavier University and enjoying a short-lived stint in corporate America, Rawa came on the job late in 1989, graduated from the academy, and was sent in May of the following year to Englewood, one of Chicago's most notorious and crime-ridden districts. Few neighborhoods have the reputation of Englewood—a dangerous, rough, and challenging district for both officers and residents.

"It was complete culture shock to me," he says. "I knew Englewood had a reputation from the papers and news, but it wasn't like anything I ever knew. It took me by surprise."

A dedicated student of police work, Rawa has filled his home bookshelves with a number of true crime books, Mafia tales, and criminal justice textbooks, in addition to a scrapbook of press clippings covering a variety of Chicago's high-profile cases. And while books tell the stories, the streets provide the unedited reality.

On his first day in Englewood, Rawa and his field-training officer heard a call for a medical examiner to a home in Englewood. Knowing it was a homicide, Rawa's partner took him to the address. There, Rawa viewed his first dead body (outside of a funeral home, that is).

"What struck me most was the citizens looking at it as commonplace," he says. "It's like they didn't need cable TV in their homes because every day in the neighborhood had more than cable TV could offer. I wanted to ask them, 'Isn't this the most traumatic thing you've ever seen?' But I knew what their answer would be.

"I'd see some nasty things, especially things dealing with kids. I'd see people beaten for a few dollars or for wearing the wrong color shirt. It was hard to put everything into perspective."

Rawa recalls hearing about a situation on the city's West Side in which 19 children were found alone—"living in squalor," as the press put it. Dirty diapers, roaches, and feces on the floor of the West End Avenue home.

"The media picked it up and ran with it," he says. "And I'm here saying we see this every day. The police officers come across this stuff daily—maybe not 19 kids—but kids being completely mistreated and abused. At first it's shocking, but the more time you put into this job, it's sad to say, the more you become callused by it. The uncomfortable part about being the police is that you're there after the fact. The damage has been done. There's little you can do about it."

Rawa says his initial years in Englewood revolved around learning how to do "real" police work—filing reports, handling domestic calls, surveying drug deals.

"It was more refereeing than anything," he says.

When the "real" police work hit, which Rawa estimates at under 10 percent of the job, he was ready. Such was the case on November 4, 1991, when Rawa and his partner came upon a suspected stolen car in Englewood. As they put on their lights to pull the car over, the driver took off and a chase ensued. Other police cars joined the pursuit as calls went over the radio. And, as most cops agree, the longer the chase goes, the more dangerous it becomes.

Eventually, the suspect crashed in an alley near 63rd and Wood streets. Rawa exited his squad car with gun drawn, but the suspect continued to fight, throwing his car into reverse and attempted to back over Rawa, who leaped onto the hood of his squad car and fired two shots into the suspect's car, hitting him in the arm and ending the chase.

> A trap in a car as discovered by Canine officer Bob Rawa and his dog, Sando. Thousands of dollars in cash along with pounds of marijuana were discovered as Sando sniffed the floor of the van.

Courtesy of Bob Rawa

"That was the first incident where I felt like my life could go in a snap," says Rawa as he presses his palms to his cheeks.

But then reality hit. Rawa says regret fills the mind of any officer after firing shots. Long after that particular incident, doubt remains with Rawa. "There's a lot of self-doubt, and you wonder if you're gonna get jammed up. You'll sit down at the roundtable and they'll want to know all the why's and how's. You watch a Clint Eastwood movie and he fires the shots, kills the bad guy, and then walks away. It's never that easy. Never."

Earning his stripes in Englewood, Rawa returned to the police academy as an instructor before joining the city's Canine Unit. And it's with the dogs that Rawa says he will stay.

"I'm at a point where I don't have to prove myself anymore," he says. "I've held my own. The job's been very good to me financially and I know I have security when I wake up every day. I know people on pins and needles about buyouts and layoffs and I don't have to worry about that junk. I got the life I want."

When Rawa was in the academy, a veteran officer told the recruits that their most productive days as Chicago cops would be from their first day out through their first seven years on the job. "I used to live for that adrenaline-filled police work; now, I do what the dog tells me to do," he says. "I've gotten to a point with over 15 years on the job, a family, nice house, money in my pocket. I've done it. Your perspective changes. I'm not saying you lay down and be a dog, but you're less interested in taking those great risks. I've found my niche with the dogs and this is the last stop."

Note: In 2007, Bob Rawa suddenly passed away from a brain hemorrhage. Survived by his wife and two kids, he was 42 years old.

SHARING THE JOB:
DETECTIVE JOHN FOLINO JR.

─────────────────── ★ ───────────────────

When John Folino Jr. was a first-grader at John Mills School in west suburban Elmwood Park, he faced the dilemma of show-and-tell. What to bring? What to talk about? He, of course, could bring his baseball glove, his favorite toy, a gift from a family trip. But Folino decided on something altogether different, and that decision, made by an energetic six-year-old, determined his life's path.

Young John elected to bring his father, Elmwood Park police officer John Folino Sr., a motorcycle cop in the blue-collar suburb. Dad had long regaled his son with stories of chasing the bad guy and doing good, so why not share those tales with others? John's day of show-and-tell began with his father pulling up on the motorcycle and John's classmates sprinting to the window upon hearing the snarl of the engine.

The horde of first graders ventured outside to meet John Folino Sr. They asked to see his handcuffs, to touch his badge. They wanted to be picked up and put on the motorcycle and pleaded for rides that, unfortunately, could never come. They demanded stories and begged for a glimpse into the copper's life.

In the background, young John Folino Jr. stood proud. His dad was a hit.

"That's when I knew I wanted to be the police," says the 29-year-old Folino today. "The degree of honor and respect I saw my father get, I wanted that, too."

So junior matched senior's footsteps, just as he promised he would that day in first grade. And these days, John Folino Jr. has earned respect and honor of his own.

─────────────────── ★ ───────────────────

Among all the sights common to Chicago Police work, entering in the middle of a felony is a rarity. And yet that is what John Folino and his partner encountered on the morning of December 26, 2003.

Working midnights in the West Side's 15th District, Folino turned a corner with his partner onto Maypole and La Crosse avenues. Eight men sat in line on the curb while two men stood above them with guns drawn and pointed. An armed robbery was in progress.

At the sight of the police squad, the robbers ran and the officers pursued. Quickly catching the culprits, Folino heard words that shook his being and sent his mind racing.

"I'm the police," one man said. "I'm the police."

Sure enough, each man had a badge—one from Harvey and the other from Ford Heights, a pair of south suburbs infiltrated with crime of their own. For the first time in his career, John Folino was lost.

The Blue Line reaches from cities to towns, urging officers to extend a degree of professional courtesy from one to the next. It doesn't mean you let officers off the hook when they do wrong, but it does mean you offer them the opportunity to get everything out in the open right then and there; you afford them the benefit of the doubt and they, in return, should furnish you with the truth. But at this moment, the line between professional courtesy and criminal activity blurred for Folino. He looked at his partner and pleaded for guidance. In time, however, he turned where he often went for straight talk and counsel.

With order restored, Folino called his father, a retired cop from Elmwood Park, a hard-working, predominantly Italian suburb immediately west of the city. And John Folino Sr., as he had many times before, provided the words his son most desperately needed. He offered perspective and gave clarity to the line that appeared hazy for his son— Where did the line between professional courtesy and crime exist? John Folino Sr. held the answer and passed it along.

In words that still ring in the younger Folino's ears, his father said, "John, there's no such thing as a crooked cop; you're either a cop or you're not. There's no giving breaks."

And on that day professional courtesy evaporated. There was no such thing as hearing them out or letting them talk without hands cuffed behind their backs—only the law, the cops, and the criminals. And no police badge would convince either Folino otherwise.

"I told him these guys were thieves," says the elder Folino, who remembers his son's call that day with detail and precision. "They're a slap in the face to real cops. They're the kind who bring suspicion down on all of us who work our butts off in the streets."

As the story played out, Chicago Police arrested a third suburban officer and discovered the trio had committed robberies throughout the Chicagoland area, all while continuing police work for their respective departments.

"I immediately reacted just as my father reacted," said John Jr. "When they ran, I knew they had to be dirty. They obviously weren't there for the reason I was there. In catching them, we helped to clear up a lot of crime in both the city and suburbs."

At 6'5", 250 pounds, John Folino Jr. is a cop with street smarts, intellect, and passion to complement his linebacker frame. For three years in the 15th District, Folino was among the top officers in the Chicago

➢ *Well before his stint in the citywide Gang Intelligence Unit and his most recent move to detective, Chicago Police officer John Folino Jr. spent the first years of his career in the 15th District's Austin area, one of Chicago's most storied neighborhoods. Though the Austin district covers under four square miles, it remains one of Chicago's most active police districts. (In October 2005, the Austin district moved from its longtime cramped stationhouse on Chicago Avenue to a modernized site on Madison Avenue.)*

Courtesy of Daniel P. Smith

Police Department for arrests, a sign of his assertive nature, his innate ability to sense that something is awry, and his constant presence on the street.

He was a natural cop, an inquisitive youngster dreaming of police work. Folino followed the path of his father and both grandfathers into law enforcement and is now himself followed by his younger brother, Tony, who works in Chicago's 10th District. When his father would arrive home from work, John, even at six years old, would notice minute details—his father's gun holster unbuckled, his name badge crooked. And young John would plead for explanations, answers to the inaccuracies.

"I was always interested to know," says Folino. "I'd ask [my father] about anything that would feed my hunger to know about his work."

John Folino Jr. joined the Chicago Police Department in 1999 at the age of 23. Upon leaving the Chicago Police Academy, Folino was sent to the West Side's Austin district, an area within minutes of Folino's childhood grounds in the adjacent Elmwood Park suburb.

Once a community bustling with middle-class families, Austin has fallen on hard times, becoming one of Chicago's most impoverished and crime-ridden areas. At the local high school, over 90 percent of the students come from low-income households while nearly one-third of students drop out before earning their diploma. Education, unfortunately, plays a secondary role to survival. And although the Austin district is Chicago's third smallest, covering less than four square miles, it remains among the city's most active for police calls. Consistently, citywide units are dispatched to the 15th District to provide a more substantial police presence and assist the local district's work.

For John Folino, the 15th District served as the classroom setting for his Chicago Police education. He studied the officers around him, seeking to learn from their experiences and insight—much the same way he continues to do with his father. Consequently, Folino began to establish his own police identity and shape a genuine copper's life.

"I was fortunate right off the bat to work with so many good officers with different styles. I could pull the good and bad from each and attempt to make myself the best officer I could be," he says.

"The academy can only teach you so much, but street sense is so different. You learn when people are getting ready to run—it's a jerk in their body, a look in their eyes, and you begin to tell from their body language, their mannerisms. Now, because I wanted to learn so much at the beginning, I can drive down the street and tell who's got the drugs, who's got the money, who's the security. All that stuff is engrained in me now and I'll never lose it. Just like riding a bike, I'll never forget it."

Despite his imposing frame, Folino holds a subtle charm. Gracious in his manners, Folino extends a smile frequently and maintains a composed demeanor. He'll revert to the "des" and "dos" that can mark the Chicago vernacular, but turn in an instant to a discussion of philosophical police issues, sounding at once tenacious and refined, a byproduct of his intellect and experience. Recently, Folino earned his MBA from St. Xavier University—"Hey, the city paid for it," he says, "and I'd be a fool not to take a free education"—and now considers returning for a second advanced degree. To be certain, no one could criticize Folino for being unmotivated.

"The big thing with Chicago is the opportunity. You can move districts, go to the Mounted Unit, Marine Unit, narcotics, there's got to be at least a hundred different units," says Folino. But soon he returns to his initial motivation for joining the job and pursuing his work with such commitment: "My father, he never had this type of opportunity; it just wasn't there in his small department. I owe it to him to take advantage of every opportunity I have."

And so for John Folino Jr. an indirect part of his work as a Chicago Police officer is making his father proud, doing things the right way, and being a cop of integrity and skill. It's like that for so many Chicago officers, so many who share the job with loved ones.

"In doing myself proud," says Folino, "by advancing in the department, by doing my job the right way, my father appreciates that and he gets to be a part of my law enforcement experience."

Folino and his father talk daily, as much a result of Folino's single life as his father's inquiring mind. Six years into young Folino's job, John Sr. remains a guiding presence and supportive force, never missing his son's police honors or advancement graduations, including Folino's recent promotion to detective in 2005

"Anything to do with the police department and he's there no matter what," says Folino of his father.

While years ago father fed stories to the son, it's now junior sharing the stories with senior, the younger Folino meeting the retired cop's hunger for action-packed tales set on Chicago's streets.

"Every day I have a story for [my father], but my story always turns into his story. Everything evolves into his experience," says Folino with a laugh. "My dad really enjoys and misses the law enforcement world. It's a common ground we share and he understood it. It's brought us closer together."

The lessons he learned from his father long ago remain with him today. His father told him as a youngster that appearance commands respect and throughout young Folino's days of wearing a police uniform, days long passed given his advancement through the ranks, Folino always had his pants and shirt creased perfectly.

"Some of the guys would bust me up about it," he says, "but I never thought of doing it another way."

Folino's father also instilled the idea of integrity in him, a thought eerily present in Austin when Folino encountered the armed robbery in progress. His father once told him that law enforcement officers sit one step closer to going to jail, perhaps a reference to the old *Honeymooners* line: "When you work in the sewers, it's hard not to get dirty."

"There's that expectation," says Folino, "that we officers should know better. We have to maintain our integrity on this job."

And as Folino arrived on the scene that winter day in 2003, his father was with him, as much a part of the job as ever, as crucial to his son as ever before. And Folino Jr. did everything just right. Plenty to make dad proud.

PART 4

POLICE WORK:
THE PERSON, THE LIFE,
AND THE SPIRIT

────────────────★────────────────

Every man is vulnerable to life's random horrors.
—*Newsweek* reporter, October 1966

I wish I had time to stop and go into each individual case. I'd say, "Hey, listen, what's your problem at home? How many kids you got? Are you working? Got a job? How are you and your wife getting along?" I'd ask all that kind of thing. But hell, you wouldn't have no time to do no work if you did that.
—Chicago Officer Ernie Cox in *Cop!*
A Close-up of Violence and Tragedy

While all cops work the street to solve cases, some cops, especially beat cops and undercover cops, inhabit the street. And the street inhabits them. What they see on the street, their knowledge that the landscape the rest of us see, is actually a backdrop for the ludicrous and hideous dramas, changes them.
—Connie Fletcher, *Pure Cop*

The cop's world allows him little time for working out reasonable conclusions about his work. If he is lucky enough to return home physically unharmed, at the end of his daily tour of duty, he still must repair his emotional equipment to be able to go through the ordeal the following day. In the social turbulence of our time the cop is often simplified—

labeled the villain or the victim of individual events.
　　　　　　　　　　　　—L.H. Wittemore, *Cop! A Close-*
　　　　　　　　　　　　　　　　up of Violence and Tragedy

　　The terrorist and the policeman both come from the
same basket.
　　　　　　　　　　　—Joseph Conrad, *The Secret Agent*

---------------------------------★---------------------------------

Here's the scene: A former Chicago Police officer stares at the ground before him and offers, "One thing you learn is that the madness doesn't need you. It goes on whether you're there or not."

It's a scene repeated elsewhere, the Chicago cop's recognition that the tumult of street life continues regardless of police efforts and idealistic aims. In many ways, it's also a realization of one's importance and value to the city, a frustrating nod to the fact that the urban police officer makes dents in the armor of street warfare, yet rarely unmasks enough of the street's knights to bring a just conclusion. In L.H. Whittemore's chronicle of police life, *Cop! A Closeup of Violence and Tragedy,* one officer puts it this way: "Sometimes I think of the ghetto as a large mountain of sand, and I'm down there at the bottom with a little shovel. And I look up, and it ain't moving."[1]

Former Chicago Police Officer Gina Gallo provides even more direct words in *Armed and Dangerous: Memoirs of a Chicago Policewoman*: "Either from failed expectations or unrealistic goals or just a sharp dose of reality, the day comes when you know, in spite of your best efforts, that your life, and your work, will never equal your dreams."[2]

Frankly, that moment—the one in which officers note their sometimes trivial role—survives as a frightening sight to witness, the moment in which our city's protectors recognize their powers extend only as far as their waking hours, and even then their force is limited or—worse— compromised by outside factors. Despite the swagger the police star often signifies, Chicago officers are neither immortal nor unshakable; they are human, in need of sleep, and capable of feeling the rawness of emotions. In one sense, you want to extend your hand and offer support; in another, you want to slap their faces and plead for a return to their original idealism, one's most righteous hopes to defeat crime. For many

Chicago officers, however, reality lands a fierce uppercut; indeed, the madness of the streets knows neither hours nor seasons nor furloughs. Its pace continues over February's icy ground just as it does in the humidity and scorch of July. Though slowed at times, the madness never comes to a definitive halt. And still, many Chicago officers remain with shovel in hand, tossing sand over their shoulders. Looking up.

The Officer's Spirit

In the lives of many Chicago officers, the street enters the mind right after academy graduation and, in time, brings varying degrees of commotion to the rest of their lives. Some turn to the bottle, others to solitude or spirituality. Some find comedy the necessary antidote; others discover cynicism as the medicine of choice. Remember that time does not always erase the darkest of memories— many persist in both sleeping and waking hours. There are some officers who refuse to take defeat, adapting to the confrontations while holding a personal mission close to their bulletproof vest. Others, however, cower before the seemingly impossible nature of it all, admitting that there's

> *Chicago's streets contain more than weeds sprouting from the asphalt, gate-covered doors and rail lines leading to unknown destinations. The city's streets contain a reality that, to borrow Father Tom Nangle's words, "reshapes souls."*
Courtesy of Daniel P. Smith

little they can do and then acting as such.

The inherent personal challenges of the job were noted as early as the late nineteenth century when Chicago officers formed fraternal societies (the Policemen's Benevolent Association in 1877; the Chicago Patrolman's Association in 1915; and the Policemen's Benevolent and Protective Association in 1936), each springing from the notion that the only ones who might understand the inner turmoil the job often brings would be other officers.[3] Such ideas remain prevalent today as the inner circles of many officers contain as many colleagues as outsiders, a fact most often created by shared experiences and schedules.

Yet, one thing remains certain throughout the decades—the life of the Chicago cop, an existence containing both terror and triumph, changes an individual. After years with the "Power of God" on their hips and the furor of criminals before them, a cop is rarely the same. Reality in Chicago includes bureaucracy, despondent children, intricate gangs, wavering justice, and the consistent struggles of humanity to push ahead in a life holding little promise. "That's what cops are supposed to do," says Gallo, "protect and serve, but not to process the horror that's all around us."[4]

We ask cops to be emotionally detached while simultaneously hoping they demonstrate superhuman traits when necessary. We want them to check emotions and memories at the district's doors, leaving behind what they carry in their hearts, so that they may act objectively in their work. Yet, we also demand they handle the most tenuous of situations—moments in which the rest of us might cower—with composure and courage. In Chicago, most officers endure a continuous stream of calls, many dealing with violent acts, drugs, gangs, and desperation. In many cases, the officers themselves become victims in social battles too often lost. An officer arrives to calm the situation, but he cannot repair the damage. Then, as the officer's career moves forward, research suggests it adapts to shifting roles, transitioning from eager rookie—"full of piss and vinegar," Chicago cops might say—to elder statesman, willing to pass on the excitement in favor of the security and safety he has earned.

Chicago and the Police

Further complicating matters in Chicago, perhaps even rushing the role changes, is the pinch of politics on departmental matters, a relationship long etched in the city's history. In 1861, for instance, Mayor

➤ *Chicago Police officers assist and await assignment at the* S.S. Eastland *disaster on July 24, 1915.*
The Eastland *disaster, a result of the ship tipping over on the Chicago River's south bank, witnessed*
the deaths of 841 passengers and four crewmembers. Police officers often work in the face of tragedy
and disaster, some recorded in print and on newscasts and others never again mentioned.

Courtesy of collection of James T. McGuire

John Wentworth, a man who once told voters, "You can either vote for
me for mayor or go to hell," dismissed all 1500 members of the police
department in one night, leaving the city without a police staff from
midnight to 10 A.M. on March 27, 1861.[5] Despite the passage of civil
service regulations in 1895, politicians successfully maintained control
over the police—with influence over assignments and promotions. In
1931, a commission investigating police organization urged the police
commissioner to leave his office in City Hall, an office that sat one door
down from the mayor's. Doing this, the commission argued, would help
curb the political influence so present in the city's police matters. (The
superintendent's City Hall office, however, stayed put until the reign of
Orlando W. Wilson three decades later.) Well into the twentieth century,
patrol members were forced by city administrations to distribute partisan
election materials as voting day neared, thereby setting the early precedent
of police serving as instruments of the political machinery.[6] Adding to
the troubles was the politician's awareness that making friends—saloon
owners, labor union chiefs, racketeers, and gamblers among them—often
churned out successful campaigns. Police, therefore, faced pressure from

the political ward machines to do their job well enough to be honest but not well enough to be moral. "The Chicago Police Department has borne the brunt of the attack from the underworld and the upperworld alike," wrote a civic commission studying the department in 1931. "In the end, its members have had to ally themselves with one side or the other."[7]

Rumor holds that Chicago Police superintendents submitted resignation letters at the time of their appointments, a sure sign that their jobs could be vanquished at the mayor's will.[8] Upon assuming the superintendent's post in 1920, Charles Fitzmorris soon dismissed over 30 slacking officers, increased criminal arrests, raided gambling joints, and began penning a merit system. His efforts were stalled soon—an election neared and Big Bill Thompson needed the votes. Superintendent Francis O'Neill, who served in the top-cop role from 1901 to 1905, said of his tenure: "Every man knows how to manage a woman until he gets married. I had some ideas myself until I got to be chief, and then, like the man who gets married, I found out."[9]

When crusading (but acting) police superintendent Joe DiLeonardi attacked the Outfit's gambling dens and threatened business in the late 1970s, politics once again intervened in the pursuit of vice. First Ward Alderman Fred Roti, once labeled with the campaign slogan "Vote for Roti and nobody gets hurt" by *Chicago Tribune* newsman Bob Davis, allegedly ordered Chicago Mayor Jane Byrne to fire DiLeonardi or risk the municipal unions shutting down business. Joe D soon thereafter arrived at a new assignment deep on the South Side. Richard Brzeczek, described as a go-along guy, gained the deserted top-cop post and Bill Hanhardt, a notorious copper who would later be convicted in a $5 million jewelry theft ring, also climbed the ladder on Roti's word. Suddenly, the Chicago officer stood between the duty to control vice and exile to the edge of the city; others, meanwhile, climbed the organizational ladder with a mix of blindness and buffoonery.

A decade before Byrne's removal of DiLeonardi for his hunt on crime, politics played a crucial role in a defining historical event—the 1968 Democratic National Convention. Author Frank Kusch, whose *Battleground Chicago* revisits the city in 1968, argues that Mayor Richard J. Daley placed his department in a position to fail. According to Kusch, Daley sent out questionable edicts to assert his power over the city as delegates and demonstrators converged on Chicago.

"I got the sense from most men that they weren't comfortable with their roles during convention week," said Kusch of his talks with dozens of Chicago officers. "They were put on a stage they weren't ready for and weren't happy with what they had to do."

The city and county judicial system, meanwhile, has also served a target of ire from officers, both past and present, prompting former Chicago officer Jack Muller to contend that the one thing ruining our society is the "American system of injustice."[10] Today's officers grumble about a lax legal system too often affording criminals fifth, sixth, and seventh chances. "Arrested yesterday, out today," contend many frustrated officers. While a variety of highly publicized cases, such as former Circuit Court Judge Frank Wilson fixing a case to acquit alleged mob hit man Harry Alleman in 1977, tug on the public's psyche just as much as the officers', the daily grind of working a case, making an arrest, and attempting to bring a suspect to justice frequently proves a process with less than satisfying results. Officers recognize that, although they may secure the criminal, justice does not always follow.

"It doesn't take long for that system of 'justice' to break a cop's heart," wrote Muller in his memoirs, *I, Pig*.

"And after his heart goes, it isn't a very big step to bend his integrity. . . . One day he realizes he's been giving up miles to gain millimeters."[11]

➤ *One of Chicago's most intriguing characteristics is its political culture. From mayoral powerbrokers down to influential ward heelers, Chicago neighborhoods, regardless of race or socioeconomic status, witness the political experience gain steady footing in daily life.*
Courtesy of Daniel P. Smith

The Officer's Soul

Yet, the potential corruption of a cop's values is only one small part of how the injustice of the street seeps into officers' lives; many fall victim to what they see and feel each day. A declining faith in humanity, for instance, stands as one of the most unfortunate losses incurred by officers. As former Officer Muller once said, "Police work isn't an eight-hour thing. You take it home with you. You take it home with you to the point where you feel so depressed about what's happening and how impossible it seems to change the system that you really wonder if it's worth going back the next day."[12]

And still, today's Chicago officers, just as those before them, return the next day and the days after. (The spirit and resolve of some is broken beyond repair, concede some Chicago officers. "It's the sad reality of the job that some coppers say it ain't worth it," says one former Chicago officer. "But they keep collecting that paycheck while the rest of us are one man down.") With sincere objectives still in mind, many officers take to Chicago's streets intent on performing their job, sacrificing a part of their being in the process—a high price to pay for a middle-class civil service job.

Over three decades ago, a study appearing in the *Journal of Police Science and Administration* showed that "police work becomes one of the few jobs which has a potent adverse effect on the total life of the worker."[13] Though nearly two generations have passed since the study's release, time that prompted additional investigations on the nature of police work, little has changed in the relationship between the officer's work and personal life. Rotating shifts, the fragmented nature of police work, danger, fear, and consistent exposure to people in pain represent a sample of the inherent stressors in police work. Couple such stressors with the bureaucratic nature of police work, a general lack of public support for officers, and ineffective court and rehabilitation programs, and it becomes clear why the weight of the job rests heavy on so many officers.

"Most cops . . . had become hardened, their hearts empty. They were no longer capable of worry or outrage at the atrocities. . . . Either extreme was too dangerous," writes Robert Blau in *The Cop Shop*.[14]

Subsequently, the cop often encounters serious emotional and physical issues, including alcohol and drug abuse, suicide, and family problems. The social drinking common in police circles, for instance, tugs at high-risk individuals. Under the direction of then-superintendent Fred Rice, a testing of nearly 2000 Chicago officers in 1984 through 1985 found 4.2 percent with

> ➤ *As Chicago's Area 4 Police Headquarters can attest, the city often witnesses police and courts heading in different directions.*
> Courtesy of Daniel P. Smith

a chemical dependency.[15] From 1977 to 1979, 20 current or retired Chicago Police officers committed suicide, five times the rate of Chicago's other citizens, and one of the department's closely guarded secrets.[16] Marital and family life, meanwhile, are often hindered by odd schedules, emotional drain, and a general hardening of the heart. Though many contend that the job does not directly cause such issues, the stress of police work, combined with the culture of the department and nature of the job, frequently accelerates such negative outcomes. While services exist to counter such issues, including an employee assistance program, many officers don't seek assistance because of denial, stubbornness, and resistance to being judged.

"Most people are reluctant to get counseling and police even more so," says Rory Gilbert, a police counselor for over 20 years. "There's a macho mentality prevalent in the police department that breeds an avoidance to help, even with those who need it most."

Our Chicago and Theirs

The truth: there are two Chicagos—the one most citizens see (ethnic neighborhoods, gentrification, church steeples, and hot dog stands) and the one police see (wearied home lives, shattered spirits, and the far-reaching effects of drugs, gangs, and violence within each neighborhood). There is a depth to the police experience that transcends casual observation and lends itself to a more intimate, thorough, and private understanding of the city and its people. The police see the world that is all around us, yet often invisible to us; they see Chicago as most of us cannot because theirs is a world demanding an exhaustive knowledge that exceeds simple recognition. They know what a fresh design of graffiti art means and what often spurs a 10-year-old to play lookout on a drug corner. A former Chicago officer describes the city as one towering skyscraper, each floor containing its own unique element of society with only the police officer claiming access to every inch of the building. While so many of us know crime in numbers or as items on the local news, police wrestle with the sickness every day. The public reads the headlines; the police live the stories—with no censors or filters to create distance. In some instances, as history shows us, the cops themselves become carriers of the disease—greed, power, money, and fear all capable villains in capturing the soul.

"The challenge for the officer is that he has to play to a higher set of standards," says late officer Bob Rawa. "When a cop gets busted for a DUI, it makes the news because the cop is supposed to be above it. The cop, though human, should know better."

> *Chicago's first courthouse (1848) stands in front of the "calaboose," the city's log house jail located at Randolph and Clark streets. To hear both past and current officers tell it, police and the criminal courts have suffered from a disconnect throughout much of the city's history.*
Courtesy of the Chicago Public Library, Special Collections and Preservation Division

> *The Chicago Police Department's Employee Assistance Program (E. A. P.) has long been an active force in guiding police through difficult life situations. Outside organizations such as St. Michael's House, which occupied this Adams Street building until the E. A .P. 's takeover in early 2006, provided similar assistance away from the city's internal group, affording officers an external outlet for their issues.*
>
> Courtesy of Daniel P. Smith

In 1969, one year after Chicago and its police department came under fire for their handling of the Democratic Convention, author L.H. Whittemore published his study of police life and its juxtaposition with the officer's personal life. In his introduction to *Cop! A Closeup of Violence and Tragedy*, Whittemore shows that police work resides on the edge of social conditions, arguing that police conduct and behavior stand as a reflection of our society and values. If police should falter, Whittemore writes, then we should correct their conduct while simultaneously evaluating our own conscience. Whittemore's words urge reflection of both citizen and officer, pushing each to examine the pressures, realities, and experiences challenging our lives, beliefs, and actions. His argument does not seek to exonerate police nor to pass blame to other parties, but rather to implore a public understanding of police officers' lives, a sense of empathy, and a recognition that the police are no different than us; they merely stand closer to the line that separates good from evil—teetering on a tightrope even—and, therefore, any fall often results from a simple misstep at a time when the room for error is minimal.

To be certain, cops' professional lives bleed into their personal lives—no matter how strict a divide they seek to maintain. The cop's life is one, says former officer Gina Gallo, "tough on your body, bad for your soul, murder on your heart."[17] The two lives remain connected, bound by service and struggles, hours and hopes. Who one is and who one becomes after years on the job cannot be separated. The officer's being—his make-up, values, and perceptions—often affects police work just as police work often affects the officer

In the following chapters are stories that illustrate this truth. Beth Russell, a sergeant who witnessed her job influencing her daughters' lives; Jim Rohrlack, an end-of-the-line detective who walked 12 steps after murder; Sergeant Joe Barnes, an African-American officer who rejects discussion of skin color in favor of his human responsibilities; Mike Cummins, a detective who retains his faith amid the upheaval of street life; and the spiritual lead, Father Tom Nangle, who mixes humor and grit to offer perspective. Each, in his or her own way, has changed, gaining thicker skin and a more resolute spirit. As such, these officers are different today than yesterday—as mothers and fathers, as friends and lovers, as brothers and sisters, as husbands and wives. Upon an officer's return home from the day's shift, the shoes and jacket may remain at the door, but the pulse of the street continues its beat in both the mind and soul. It is the rare cop (some would say the disconnected one) who says his concern over police work finishes at shift's end and, more accurately, means it. Thoughts of work can intrude on home life at any time—they just as easily interrupt midnight hours in front of a television or staring at the ceiling as they haunt morning moments gazing into a cup of coffee or watching children as they ready for school.

To be certain, Chicago remains a city filled with officers who carry the job in their minds and hearts, affecting both today's moves as well as tomorrow's. They encounter the madness each day.

Shovel in hand.

Looking up.

SEPARATE WORLDS:
SERGEANT BETH RUSSELL

---★---

Christmas Day in Rogers Park, the Far North Side neighborhood brimming with diversity and character, placed Beth Russell in a 24th District beat car, awaiting the opportunity to head home for some Christmas dinner herself. "Everything's quiet before Christmas dinner. It's only after that the shouting starts," reminds Russell.

Responding to a call of a man sitting alone on a park bench, Russell arrived at the neighborhood park to see the older man battered by the cold—blue cheeks and slumbering words. "All he kept saying was, 'I used to live around here,'" says Russell. "But we couldn't find anyone who knew the man."

Pulling out his wallet for identification, the man displayed an address in Glen Ellyn, a distant western suburb with upper-class roots. Police surveyed the area looking for a car with a Glen Ellyn sticker and soon landed upon a purple Ford Fiesta in immaculate condition. As it turns out, the man, who suffered from dementia, had escaped to Rogers Park in a dreary haze.

Chicago Police called the Glen Ellyn Police Department and said they would be bringing the man back to his home address. And off Beth Russell and a colleague went, both missing their Christmas dinners, Russell tucked in behind the wheel of the purple Ford that followed her colleague and the elderly man in the Chicago squad. When they arrived at the man's Glen Ellyn home, a suburban officer waited outside, and the police escorted the man upstairs. They found his personal phone book and called his caregiver, who abandoned her own holiday gathering to be with the man.

"There was nobody there for that man, but the police were there for him. We saved him from being a victim. And I didn't so much mind missing Christmas dinner for that," she says with a smile.

"You know what that guy kept asking me when we got him home? He kept saying, 'Am I in trouble? Am I in trouble?'

"I could only look at him and say, 'No, sir, you're not in trouble. You're home.'"

———————————————★———————————————

There are two distinct worlds many of Chicago's officers inhabit: the world of cartoon-themed nightlights, pastel-painted walls, fresh milk in the refrigerator, and green lawns; and the world of urine-stenched stairwells, dented doors, and people staggering through their own human existence— some permanently and some only temporarily.

And, believe it or not, discerning which world is the "real" one can sometimes be a difficult task. Beth Russell's one of the lucky ones; she'll tell you as much—she noticed the challenge early and made the necessary distinctions.

At midnight, Russell may have found herself searching a home for drugs, with rodents scurrying past her feet and the stench of hard liquor filling the room. Hours later, however, she would arrive at her Northwest Side home and flick on a light switch to see her daughters snuggled in beds of freshly washed sheets. Their heads smelling of fruity shampoo, the girls wore matching pajama tops and bottoms. All Beth Russell could do was shake her head and wonder. "Which world is the real one?" she'd ask. "Which one is real?"

Today, a cool October morning in 2005 that encourages full breaths of the city's crisp air, Beth Russell sports a pink cardigan, polka-dotted socks, and a beaming smile. Her North Side condo is bright and inviting.

She offers the typical greetings and rushes toward the unit's rear, saying, "This is what sold me." She steps onto her fifth floor balcony and embraces a green landscape and open skies, an exception from the concrete that graces much of Chicago's urban space. She inhales the calm autumn air and accepts the splash of light today's sky delivers. She is both at peace and in her element—in her real world, at least the one she's decided to make her real one. For her, it's now a world with active grandchildren, white walls stenciled with ivy trim, and handmade sitting chairs carved from a Wisconsin tree.

The real world, Beth Russell was told during her first months on the job, is the one she lives in. That simple. And the real world she lives in calls her mom or grandma, not officer.

➤ *A sampling of the diverse life present in Rogers Park, in which foreign languages dominate storefronts and sidewalk conversations and where the push of American commercialization achieves only modest results. Current Chicago Police Sergeant Beth Russell names her time in a Rogers Park beat car among her career's most memorable periods.*

Courtesy of Jennifer Sisson Photography

Throughout her 23 years at the Chicago Police Department, Russell has been committed to seeing that the distinct worlds she inhabits remain separate places. She's a cop and she's a mother, and although the two may touch, she has resisted the collision—the interminable depletion of humanity that has made too many iron-hearted at times and jaded at others.

That's why Russell always washed her hands when she arrived home from work. A routine act with an unquestionable symbolism, Russell's action survives as one of the simple things we do in life to convince ourselves that such a habitual deed can erase the day's dirty work—like gurgling mouthwash to forget the presence of alcohol. Still, the hand-washing served a necessary step for Russell, a chance to remove the worries of one world to concentrate on the demands of another.

"I didn't want what had touched the street to touch my children," she admits.

Beth Russell encountered the dual role faced by so many Chicago officers—that of parent and that of cop. An existence in two distinct worlds, urging the individual at the center to decide where one will stop and the other will begin.

"One thing I've found is that the same hands that will arrest someone are the same ones that cook and change diapers," says Russell.

"When you're a police family," she continues, "you know that officer can get hurt, but you can't let it consume your family life. By the same token, your family life cannot be part of your police life. It's your job. Your family can't play into it when you're working."

At home, Russell faced the reality and struggle of a household with two Chicago cops, her then-husband a cop working inside the detective's division. Her new career required an uneasy adjustment for her two school-aged girls.

"It's okay when dad was a cop, but not mom," says Russell. "Their father had been a cop since they could remember, but it was more difficult to accept me as a cop because I was the center of their world. That transition from civilian mom to officer mom was a difficult one. I thought the girls were old enough to handle it, but I don't know if they ever liked it.

"I always felt that structure and schedule was hard on them. There was a time I was stuck on 4–midnight's early on, and I remember calling and the girls would be crying for me to come home."

To ease the adjustment, Russell would not discuss police work at home—"Well, only the silly stuff," she concedes. "It helped them see some

> *A brick wall outside the Rogers Park 24th District station leaves little room to question the building's occupant. The far North Side district boasts one of Chicago's most diverse and varied constituencies.*
Courtesy of Jennifer Sisson Photography

of the job."—and demanded her husband do the same.

"Home was always for the little, curly haired girls. They got to talk, not us," she says. Still, she cannot help but think her job influenced her own children's lives.

"It's a job that affects childhood. They were under the microscope more. I became strict, and that was entirely because I saw what was out there. I was more aware," Russell says. "Now that the girls have grown up, they say I was hard on them, but they see it was for a reason. They have no desire to be the police whatsoever though. They do their own work from the heart."

At 54 years old, Russell's face is vibrant and young, with a smile that shines with grace and warmth. She's reflective in her thoughts and has achieved the balance of motherhood and police work—placing each in its proper perspective, assigning each its necessary time and space.

Though her Chicago Police career began more out of inquiry than desire, Russell has nonetheless arrived at a job she loves, one that has made her a better person in so many ways.

"When I got into the academy, I told myself I'd give it a month and that if I didn't like it, I'd quit. But this job's been good to me," she says. "In the old days if I had seen a fight, I would've run away. Now, I run into it because it's instinct. I'm not afraid to take the initiative now; I have confidence in myself, especially in situations in which I would've been mush before."

After taking the test in July of 1981, Russell entered the academy the following summer and was assigned in December to the city's 20th District, which governs Chicago's Near North Side. After six years of loving the work, she accepted a move further north to Rogers Park in early 1989, where she stayed for the next decade.

"It was the happiest time of my career being in a beat car," she says of her first 16 years on the job. "You got that immediate interaction with people."

In January of 1998, she took the sergeant's exam and by July earned the promotion, soon after returning to the 20th District. Today, she serves as a sergeant in Area 3's Detective Division, an area covering much of the city's North Side.

"I love it," she says of the work she was at first reluctant to embrace. "This job allows us to get into some people's lives and, hopefully, make a difference.

"I always wanted to be a nurse, and in this job I get to put some Band-Aids on, heal some wounds, and give a shot of praise. It's a good and worthy thing. You're helping poor souls, sometimes even from themselves."

Russell arrived at that realization early in her career—the idea that good could be done while she monitored the streets. Upon leaving the scene of a finished bar fight, Russell's partner asked her why she had a frown on her face.

"I told him I should be home with my kids, not involved in this chaos. But he looked at me and said, 'Think of all the people who've never dealt with the police. You can bring a different angle to it. There's a lot of good you can do out here.'"

And so Russell carried that attitude with her. She began to discover that the same traits she developed as a mother—patience, understanding, and compassion among them—could also make her a good cop. (She even admits to activating her "mom" voice on occasion, the commanding tone that halts nearly all situations.)

When frigid winters descended upon the city, Russell remembers that many of the school crossing guards would call in sick, requiring Russell and other beat cops to fill the role. Working the intersection of Sheridan and Gunnison avenues, Russell encountered a father taking his two girls to school, each of the youngsters clothed only in short-sleeved t-shirts. The father, who only recently arrived in Chicago with his family from Southeast

Asia, told Russell through an interpreter that he was going to register the girls at school. Russell sprinted into action.

"It just broke my heart to see them shivering like that," she says. "I went home and gathered winter clothes my kids had outgrown along with some from neighbors and went to that crossing the next day with two shopping bags full of clothes."

Other officers on Russell's watch saw her actions and soon began bringing their children's outgrown clothing to the school office.

"It gave me such great satisfaction," says Russell. "I don't know if that's law enforcement work, but our job isn't all law enforcement. You just try to make a positive experience somewhere."

Still, Beth Russell could not, in her capacity as an officer, ignore the fact that she was also a mother—the instincts and realities of that world often emerging an asset in many dilemmas. Most notably, that motherly instinct, that sixth sense of pain and want, often aiding her police efforts.

On a Sunday morning in the 20th District, Russell arrived at a domestic dispute, often among the most uncomfortable cases cops encounter. A mother, traveling from her South Side home, trekked up to the city's North Side with her two young boys to get money from the boys' father. A dispute ensued and police were summoned. Russell arrived on the scene in a supervisory role to get conflicting stories from both adult parties. She noticed the boys, however, standing on the side, each trembling and tearful. She knew immediately that they had witnessed something.

"I keyed in on those kids," she says. "I saw the terror in them. I knew right away they saw something that shook them terribly."

In jittery speech, the boys told Russell that their father had tried pushing their mother out the window. The boys, meanwhile, grabbed their mother's pants to keep her from falling, an act that resulted in her pants falling below her knees and leaving the boys scared and embarrassed. Russell looked up at the ten-story building to see one window perched open without a screen. The father was taken into custody, and a squad car drove the boys and their mother back to their South Side home.

"We could show those kids that there was justice, that we could listen to their story and try to make the situation right," Russell says.

She refuses to talk of child abuse cases she has encountered throughout her nearly two dozen years on the job. The most detail she offers of any instance regards one she encountered while a sergeant in the 20th District. She tells nothing of the kids' condition, only saying that another officer told her at the visit's conclusion, "Sarge, I thought I was gonna have to hold you back."

As a mother, she can only imagine the horror the children experience, the tainted view of humanity they come to possess. All she can do, she says, is attempt to make the situation right at that moment, to provide some sense of order, calm, and comfort. Not at all that different from motherhood, the times she encountered with her own girls, journeys to find the proper footing in stressful circumstances.

At a Mother's Day mass for police officers, Russell once spoke to attendees and said she'd had the honor of being a Chicago Police officer for over two decades, but the privilege of being called mother for much longer. She reminded everyone that while the pride of being a Chicago Police officer recedes with retirement, the pride of being a mother, a parent, could never be erased. She spoke of mothers and fathers only wanting what is right and good for their children, particularly in light of the negativity an officer sees.

"Being a mom was the tougher job," she says today. Russell directs her eyes ahead, releases a breath, and confides, "I don't think being a police officer made me a better mother. That's the truth. It took me away from my kids.

"If I had a job in the private sector, I don't think it would've affected my children so much. Our work affects our children. We're a little harder on them. We ask more questions and it's because we're aware of the reality. But being a police officer did help me prepare the girls for the realities of the world. I think I taught the girls to be more aware, how to carry themselves, and they learned how not to be victims. Maybe that's a scary thing, but it's a very real thing. I certainly learned to cover more bases."

Russell later tells of the pre-work ritual she shared with her girls. Again, one of those habitual things we do to convince ourselves that distinct worlds can inherit separate spaces. "Every day when I left for work," she says, "the girls always knocked on my back to make sure I had my vest on. It was always that—a kiss and a knock on the back and I was out the door."

Out the door and away from her real world. Hours later, she would return home.

Her shoes at the door.

Her hands over the sink.

Answering to mom.

TWELVE STEPS TO A BETTER COP: DETECTIVE JIM ROHRLACK

★

St. Michael's House sits on the corner of Lake Street and Wood Avenue. Just blocks away are the United Center and the Michael Jordan statue, a tribute to athletic excellence. St. Michael's House, meanwhile, stands as a tribute to something else—resilience.

On the wall inside the front door, a small wooden frame holds a Chicago Police patch above the city's flag. Up two flights of stairs is the office of Rory Gilbert, who—with Dr. Clifton Rhead, Dennis Nowicki, and Jerry Bolger—founded The Police Assistance Center in 1987.

A non-profit agency, St. Michael's House, which sprouted from the Police Assistance Center in 2000, serves law enforcement personnel throughout the Chicagoland area—employees and their spouses from the Chicago Police Department, federal agencies, county and state departments, as well as suburban officers. Gilbert, a University of Chicago grad with an unruffled demeanor and casual look, begins speaking of the group's work as well as of his late partner, Jerry Bolger, a Chicago native and former Chicago Police officer who won his own battle against alcoholism and spent the remainder of his lifetime helping others fight theirs.

While the bulk of the cases at St. Michael's House involve relationship issues, Gilbert estimates that alcoholism is a factor in nearly 40 percent of cases. The combination, he says, of a police culture that accepts alcohol and odd schedules places many officers at risk. In his nearly two-dozen years assisting officers, Gilbert has observed his share of fights with the bottle. Some won. Some lost. In all cases, Jerry Bolger was the point man, with a combination of wits, intuition, and empathy rolled into his gritty frame.

"I think it was a part of his own recovery," says Gilbert of his late colleague. "Somehow out of his own experience he was sensitive to what was going on with others."

Jim Rohrlack was one of those people, a man who saw

in Bolger what he wanted for himself.

"Jerry could relate to people," says Rohrlack, a veteran Chicago detective now nearing retirement. "He was your garden variety drunk. And that's the reason he was so successful, that's why his program worked. People talked to him and they knew he was speaking from his heart and they knew he understood. They would see that he'd gotten better and would want that for themselves."

Jim Rohrlack tells one such story.

---------------------------------★---------------------------------

In 1978, barely one year removed from the Chicago Police Academy, Jim Rohrlack killed a man by shooting him in the head, an event that triggered his demise.

"That's when I got really macho," says Rohrlack, not a trace of pride in his statement. "I took on the persona I thought others expected of me."

Working the tact team in the Northwest Side's 16th District, one of Chicago's less disturbed areas, Rohrlack responded to "an armed robbery in progress" call at Mel's Menswear near Lawrence and Milwaukee avenues, arriving to see precisely what the call promised—a man holding a knife to the throat of the owner's son. Rohrlack and his partner repeatedly ordered the robber to drop the knife; but the robber, who appeared to be under the influence of drugs, only pulled the knife closer to the victim. And so Rohrlack fired, striking the robber in his temple.

"The first thing I thought about was losing my job," says Rohrlack. "I was 28 years old and had a young family."

Detectives, along with leadership from the district, arrived and assured Rohrlack he did the right thing. They consistently asked what they could do for him and Rohrlack was relieved that other members of the department were taking care of him as a professional and concerned for his well-being. Yet, a twisted feeling dominated his emotions—if not immediately, than surely in the aftermath.

"I didn't have a good feeling about what I did. There was no bravado whatsoever," he says.

And though a downward spiral seemed inevitable prior to the event, a tailspin quickly gained steam.

"I wasn't fine, but I went on working," he says. "They told me I could take time off, but I didn't think that was necessary. I was convinced I had to play the role of the macho cop, that I had to keep up that bravado.

"I wasn't going to show my soft underbelly, so I just stuffed a lot of it. I was not a badass, not a tough guy. All of a sudden, I did something that went that way. I thought I was coming out here to help people. But I got some 'heavy cheese,' as they say, and I wasn't processing it very well."

He soon discovered solace in the bottle, often an easy prescription to escape and dull his sharp thoughts. Although he says alcoholism was wired in his DNA, the fatal shooting accelerated the process. He repressed his emotions, resisted help, and battled his demons alone, all the while aware that he was traveling a sad, lonely road. He immersed himself in a frenetic work schedule that—outside of his police duties—included part-time jobs at a used car lot on the city's West Side and a restaurant in west suburban Cicero. By keeping on the move, he was attempting to suppress the turmoil brewing inside him.

"I wasn't going home at night; I was getting drunk," says Rohrlack, a sincere disappointment evident in his speech. "I was working all those side jobs so I could feed the disease. I had good intentions but they didn't match the actions.

"Some people asked me if I needed any counseling. I didn't see the need for that; I was a tough guy." His eyes pointed forward, he releases a gentle chuckle, a humble acceptance of the truth follows: "I wasn't."

Requesting a move out of the 16th District, Rohrlack hoped a geographical change would solve his issues.

"I stuffed everything down. I drank and drank and was getting sick of that. And I was getting sick of hearing that I did a good job, so I got out of 16," he says of his move to the city's 18th District, an area most notable for the presence of Rush Street. "But in the '70s, Rush Street was sex, booze, and rock n' roll. My

➢ *A mural inside police headquarters at 35th and Michigan pays tribute to Chicago's industrial history.*
Courtesy of Jenifer Sisson Photography

drinking only escalated."

He then moved from Loop Traffic to the West Side's 15th District, and then to the 17th District. None of the geographical changes, however, spurred a change in his habits.

During this dark time, Rohrlack also studied for the detective's exam. He points to the response of the detectives at the scene of the 1978 shooting, recalling their professionalism, their concern. So impressed was a young Rohrlack then that he swore he would be a detective someday. That lone bright spot, however, disappeared when, in Rohrlack's words, "I found out the dick's test wasn't as legit as I thought it was. People below me on the list were getting called ahead of me. I lost some zip once I found that out."

Increasingly, he took to the bottle. Before work. After work. Sometimes not making it into work.

"More and more, I was losing me," he says, a sigh and shake of the head following the statement. "I was always a guy who could leave the job behind. Instead, I was at bars trying to bury this thing; I didn't want to feel."

Rohrlack is quick to acknowledge that police work did not cause his battle with alcoholism; he would've faced the battle regardless of his career path. "Eventually, things would have spiraled this way," he tells. "The cop culture may have accelerated this, but it didn't cause it. I say that only because I was exposed to more opportunities because I was a cop. There's a dangerous combination in the cop culture that accepts drinking and also revels in the John Wayne thing. At a lot of bars, coppers roll in and everything's on the house. It can be a dangerous mix."

Raised by his grandmother because both his parents were alcoholics, Rohrlack admits trouble facing many of his life's realities. He finally realized that he had crossed the line into alcoholism; in 1982, four years after the fatal shooting, Rohrlack pursued change.

"I turned up drunk to work and just said that I couldn't live like this anymore," he says.

Rohrlack called a lieutenant who was, as the recovering cops say, "on the program." The lieutenant directed him to Jerry Bolger, the former Chicago street cop with alcoholic tales of his own to share. Later that same day, Bolger's office called Rohrlack at home.

"They told me to pack my bags and go to Lutheran General Hospital. And I did what they told me to do," says Rohrlack. "I got tired of running from myself. I didn't like what I had become."

He spent three days at Lutheran General in suburban Park Ridge before spending four weeks at Parkside Center in north suburban Mundelein. In time, Rohrlack learned about the disease of alcoholism and began to understand the issues central to his problem.

"In that process of recovery, I began to take responsibility for my actions. I began to see that I wasn't a bad person, but I was a sick person," he says. "A lot of the things I was doing were cries for help. I was 33 going on 13—immature, selfish, like the world didn't give me mine. I was angry about a lot of things.

"My life was fear-based and, of course, with that fear I became an ego-maniac with an inferiority complex. I was trying to cover up the idea that I didn't measure up." And although he's been sober for 23 years, he still says, "You never graduate from this. It's a lifelong process."

His steps to sobriety were followed in March, 1987, by his earning a detective's spot, a rank he has held in Area Four for the last 18 years. "My police career was reborn when I made detective," he says shining a grin. Now, with retirement nearing, Rohrlack enjoys his final days while also appreciating the necessary change to come.

"Things are changing," he says, "and like a lot of guys, I don't like change. It's time." Still, he'll take with him a lifetime of warm memories, friends, and experiences that have shaped his current existence. He says he always relished in department camaraderie, the bonds that joined one to another, the shared experiences that produced lasting friendships.

"Yeah," he laughs, "I'll miss the clowns but not the circus. I've got my 30 years of vaudeville and a pension."

After the laughter subsides, he recalls the time he put an addition on his former home and a group of fellow officers came over to help him knock down trees. That fellowship, says Rohrlack, is the aspect he'll miss most. "One of the greatest things about this job is the cavalry coming together. You don't get this in a lot of other professions. Many of us older coppers say that the younger guys will make more money, but they'll never have more fun."

Now 56 years old, Jim Rohrlack says he's a better man, a better cop these days. He laughs a little more. He shares his thoughts, his emotions more. He listens more and advises more. And, above all else, he empathizes more. A thin man, Rohrlack is nevertheless sturdy in stature with thick arms, a remnant of his football days at Colorado State University. "An option QB," he says pointing to a set of jagged scars on his knees. "But they don't run the option much anymore." Just one more way things have changed in Rohrlack's life.

During his dark period, Rohrlack says he would just assume no one was telling the truth as he handled investigations. The result was a distrust of humanity followed by a distaste for people. His emergence from alcoholism, however, allowed him to see police work from a different perspective, a product of learning to see himself and his life from an enhanced viewpoint.

"Once I got through my stupor and got to see where John Q. Public was coming from, I got to understand. I was able to step out of me after I had the tools to do so. I began to understand why people call the police," he says. "The people in those high-crime areas, they are people with faith and spirituality and goodness, but they're consumed by their environment. My feelings returned to me, I am now able to empathize. I still have to keep my guard, but I no longer assume that people are just lying to me. They're struggling with life the same way I struggle with life."

Sobriety, he says, allowed him to become a better Chicago cop, enriching his own life as well as those he meets.

"It made me a better cop because it made me a better human being," he says. "For once in my life, it's not all about me. And it's much more rewarding this way. Why do I listen now? Because I'm not nursing a hangover; because I'm not into myself; and because this is what I'm here for.

"I've had thieves and robbers struggling with their own addictions. I'll tell them, 'Let's forget about the crime—let's put that to the side. Let's talk about you.' Then, they'll tell me what they've been doing. They see that what comes from the heart reaches the heart. Ultimately, that's what helps me be a better police officer."

Once in a while, he'll take a walk into St. Michael's House. While Jerry Bolger's only recently passed, the spirit of the counseling center he helped shape remains intact. Officers flood in and out, each with their own baggage, their own demons to destruct. Rohrlack might stop at meetings or chat with others in the hall. Most coppers, he reminds, are more likely to go to another cop before anyone else, a sign of that shared experience extending beyond the streets. And Rohrlack stands eager to help as the situation demands.

"That officer will get back and be a more productive cop, a better person. But all I can really do is tell them what I was and what I am now. This has all been given back to me because I'm not the center of the universe anymore."

Rohrlack brings his hands together, crossing fingers with one another and allowing his palms to meet.

"I'm one of the lucky ones," he says, a grateful nod to the resurgence he's had in life. "And it's important I never forget that."

Note: In April 2006, St. Michael's House, a non-profit center unconnected to the Chicago Police Department, closed its doors as a result of underfunding.

A BLACK AND WHITE ISSUE:
SERGEANT JOE BARNES JR.

———————————————★———————————————

Joe Barnes Jr. calls it as he sees it—a ball's a ball and a strike's a strike. And the world, he says, possesses a universal strike zone.

He's relaying some life history right now. A childhood in Englewood. High school at Chicago Vocational. Life as the middle son in the Barnes family. A rather routine existence, but one with its own flair. He details his life's progression with sincerity and polish, neither admonishing nor downplaying any event.

In time, talk turns to his late father and it becomes apparent where Joe Barnes Jr. acquired his life's values. Joe Barnes Sr., a lifetime worker for the Chicago Board of Education, was an adoring husband and father to three boys. "My father was a janitor," says Barnes. "Not a custodian. Not a maintenance engineer. A janitor. He wasn't much for wordplay. He cleaned toilets, but he said it was good and honest work that put food on the table. And just like his father, Joe Barnes Jr. spent time as a janitor as well for the Board of Education before joining the Chicago Police Department. And just like his father, he isn't much for wordplay.

"I'm not the man. My father was. He stood tall and I'm just trying to," he says, a weighty sigh following the statement, an admission that Barnes recognizes the exhaustive nature of the task. He shakes his head, an action accompanied by laughter, perhaps a solitary moment to reflect on what lies ahead with his own young sons.

"I'm just trying to lead a good life for my family and me. It really is that simple."

No wordplay necessary.

———————————————★———————————————

Say the name Christopher Darden and most people remember something about him.

A middle-aged black man with wiry glasses and a sturdy stature, Darden served as the prosecuting attorney in the O.J. Simpson double-murder trial in Los Angeles—the so-called "Trial of the Century." As a result, Darden's face and name blanketed the media and he emerged—whether he wanted it or not—a recognized man. Suddenly, his past, his character, his life was on trial in the court of public opinion as much as Simpson's alleged murder consumed the L.A. courtroom of Judge Lance Ito. And some in the nation, particularly members of the African-American community, detested Darden and his actions. Shouts of "Uncle Tom" followed his steps into the courtroom each day while insults and criticism trailed behind. Why would Darden, a black man himself, want to prosecute Simpson, a fellow black man?

Darden struggled with the questions himself, laboring over his responsibilities as both a black man and a human being. Where does one end and the other begin? Do such lines even exist?

A decade later, Joe Barnes Jr., a 45-year-old African-American man, reflects on the Simpson case and, specifically, Darden. One might think Barnes, a sergeant with the Chicago Police Department, struggles with the same dilemma—the dual citizenship in two communities often at odds. Yet Barnes maintains clarity on the issue, a sense that he's living the right life—and nobody can tell him otherwise. Nobody, Barnes says, can question his motives.

"Chris got pulled into that," says Barnes without a trace of doubt in his voice. "He allowed himself to get dragged into that debate when he should have said, 'Who are you to not want me to do my job? Put your wife, your sisters, your kids out there and tell me if you want a potential murderer on the streets with them.' I know my answer." If nothing else, Joe Barnes is surely comfortable with himself, his life's path, and the choices he's made along the way.

As a seventh-grader at Yale School in the city's Englewood neighborhood, Barnes recalls a substitute teacher walking into the classroom and asking, "How many of you boys want to be police officers?" Barnes raised his hand, joining another boy in the room. "Sure, why not?" thought Barnes. "I could do that job."

The teacher, a young black woman, looked the youthful Joe Barnes

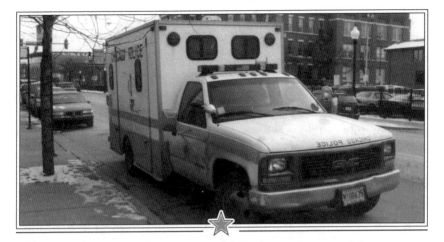

➤ *A paddy wagon sits outside Chicago's 9th District Station.*
Courtesy of Jennifer Sisson photography

in the eyes and fired another more direct question: "Why would you ever want to arrest your own people?"

Joe Barnes, born and raised in predominantly African-American Englewood, didn't answer the question then and he won't answer it now.

Looking back, he knows a prior event precipitated her question. Yet Barnes, a giant man at 6'4" and 280 pounds, sees little reason to bother with such questions. In fact, he fires back. Though his voice is soft and his demeanor calm, Joe Barnes is not one to retreat from a challenge—intellectual or otherwise.

"Who was she to ask me that question? What were her qualifications to ask me that question? And what was her stake in my answer?" says Barnes today, now a decorated 18-year veteran of the Chicago Police Department.

Barnes refuses to get pulled into semantics, refuses to discuss secondary issues when more pressing matters persist and, to be certain, refuses to stray from a well-considered personal belief structure that guides his daily life. Joe Barnes is a black man; but even more important, he is a human being. His life's mission is to do the best he can as a man. When he puts on his Chicago Police uniform, life becomes about what is good and what is bad, what is right and what is wrong, and he refuses to cower from making such calls.

Still, being aware of race—and reminded of it—is nothing new to Barnes. Born in the Englewood neighborhood in 1959, Barnes recalls his family being the third black household on the block. By the end of the 1960s, however, there were no white families left on his street near 70th and Yale.

"Things changed and they changed quick," Barnes says of Englewood in the 1960s and '70s. "You couldn't help but notice."

Barnes also recalls his early interaction with the Chicago Police. "The police not only caught you if you were up to no good, but whipped you and talked about it, too. The [Office of Professional Standards] wasn't involved," he says. "If the police told you to leave, you did, fast. I don't know if it was fear or respect, but I do know that respect is what's missing today."

In the Barnes household, education was paramount. His father and mother were high school graduates who valued strong academic achievement above all else.

"One of the most profound statements I've ever heard and one I'll take with me to my grave," says Barnes, "is my father telling me that it will one day take a high school degree to dig graves. My grandmother said it to my father and he passed it on to us boys. Both my parents made clear the fact that education would be important to us and it was an expectation that we go to college."

After graduating from Chicago Vocational High School, where he was a member of the 1976 Prep Bowl Championship football team, Barnes followed his father's footsteps and worked as a janitor for the Chicago Board of Education while simultaneously earning his credits toward an education degree at Chicago State University. It was there that Barnes first entertained serious thoughts about life as a police officer.

"I remember one of my philosophy classes at Chicago State and the professor speaking about Divine Law. Most people in law enforcement believe they're pursuing or upholding the universal laws of right and wrong. And this idea was something I knew well because it was the household I was brought up in."

Intrigued, Barnes decided to pursue law enforcement courses, and in the summer of 1985, with his younger brother and a few other neighborhood buddies in tow, took the Chicago Police test.

"My mother hated it because she wanted me to be in education," he says, "but my father was quietly pleased and proud. To this day, I regret not inviting him to my detective's graduation. I played it down, but he would have been proud and happy to be there."

In 1988, Barnes's police career began in the Pullman District at 111th Street and Ellis Avenue, an area rich in history, located on the far South Side. However, during the Reagan years, Pullman struggled economically given the absence of industry and opportunity, and crime soared.

During his first months in Pullman, Barnes's decision to join the Chicago Police Department was vindicated, and he has yet to look back. While working the wagon, Barnes received a call at 3 A.M. to go to 117th and Ada streets. In the alley, he entered a scene in which a young man was having sex with an elderly woman. Earlier, the man, who had grown up in the neighborhood, had kicked down the woman's door and pursued her. Getting to her late husband's gun, the lady attempted to shoot the assailant, but the gun would not fire. The man then took the gun, dragged the woman into the alley, and began to rape her. After arriving, Barnes quickly put the attacker into custody, and the man gave a full admission of guilt.

"I remember the woman having scratches all over her arm," says Barnes, "and I remember thinking that this is why I wanted to become an officer: to stop evil. That's not the kind of guy I want on the street with my mother or my wife. I was glad I was in the position to do that because if I wasn't there to get the guy, then there's a good chance he would've done it again."

While working in the city's Third District, Barnes recalls another case that resides deep in his memory, a situation that still disheartens him.

A man riding around in a white van grabbed schoolgirls as they returned home and then raped them. With his first victim, a 16-year-old, he did not cover her eyes. While he did show her a knife and threaten her life, his misstep allowed the police to gain an eyewitness to his physical features. With his second and third victims, a 14-year-old and 9-year-old, he realized his mistake and blindfolded both girls first. The girls, however, were able to see under the blindfold and offer police a description of the van. Chicago Police later found the man and arrested him, but the aftermath sent chills through the victims and Barnes.

The nine-year-old victim, recalls Barnes, gave him the most chilling account of the rape. Held hostage in the man's van, she heard sirens approaching and believed police were coming to her rescue; the police, however, were responding to a different call in the area. The young girl's hope false, her living nightmare continued without hesitation.

"That was most disheartening because I couldn't help her or relieve the hurt. She was hurt. She needed help. And I couldn't be there at that specific time," says Barnes, whose shaking head shows genuine frustration. "I wished I could've been there for that girl in her time of need. Here she was thinking help was coming, but it wasn't."

Equally disturbing for Barnes was the man's unwavering knowledge of his crimes. "After the nine-year-old performed oral sex on him, he gave her a piece of gum to take the taste out of her mouth. He knew he did wrong and that's what really angered me."

What bothers Barnes most is that crime and evil occurred, that the universal laws of morality went violated. The skin color of Barnes, the victims, or the perpetrators demands no mention and Barnes refuses to pay the issue lip service. For Joe Barnes Jr., the lines of crime in Chicago are clear and colorless ones.

"The city didn't hire me because I am black. They hired me because I had the qualifications. If I didn't pass the tests, if I had a felony conviction, then it wouldn't matter if I were black or white; I wouldn't be a cop in Chicago."

Barnes goes on to say that black officers enhance Chicago's police force in ways others cannot. The same, he argues, can be said for female or Latino officers. "Each group has their own comfort level with people they can communicate with. Black officers enhance the department in their own way and the same can be said of many others," says Barnes. "I've had female partners in sex crimes, and they were able to handle the situation in their own way, bringing a perspective to it that I couldn't. The truth is that most police want to do good, to be an effective part of the solution using the best tools and judgment we have."

Still, some people of all races, wish to make color an issue, something Barnes quickly rejects.

"The only question ever posed to me was the generic one by that teacher," he says. "She could not see the necessity for black officers. Anybody thinking that way is not thinking objectively. I will have people ask, 'Why are you, a black officer, arresting this black man?' Because based on the evidence I have, he did it. We all know right and wrong and we're either going to be a part of the solution or a part of the problem."

Barnes takes it further. An analytical and methodical man, he points out that no one person can speak for the black community at large. For any who wish to challenge Barnes or question his motives, his response is sincere, direct, and supported by his actions. "Whenever people want to ask me [why I'm arresting another black man], I can answer that," says Barnes. "Do you have a mother, a sister, a child out there? Then, why wouldn't you want me to do my job? Race shouldn't be the issue. It should be, do I want safer streets for my family and the people close to me?"

So if there is a black and white issue, it is not about skin color, but rather the good and evil that line Chicago's streets. And Joe Barnes knows where he stands. "Life is full of choices and I've made mine," he says. "I'm going to be on the good side and there's no doubt about that."

As Barnes sits back and glares into the distance, a flurry of activity continues along 119th Street as the darkness intrudes upon a cool spring evening. As cars and people pass, Barnes remains in steady contemplation. Later, he stands, walks out the west door of the McDonald's and stops just short of the asphalt driveway.

"You know, there's so much more to worry about in this world," he begins, "so many better things we could turn our attention to, so many better things that demand our time and effort. Talking about race—black, white, polka dot, whatever—that takes us away from the real issues we need to address. And me? I won't be distracted."

FAITH:
DETECTIVE MIKE CUMMINS

★

It's a frigid winter evening in Chicago's Rogers Park neighborhood, perhaps the city's best attempt to mimic a United Nations conference. Officer Mike Cummins arrives at a domestic dispute on Columbia Avenue to see a woman screaming wildly at a man, flailing her arms and forcing sharp movements. As Cummins approaches, another lady stops him. "I have the baby," she says. "I have the baby."

Like so many officers, Cummins steps into an unknown world, a world in which he must immediately attempt to create order amidst chaos. Additional police cars arrive, followed by the wagon. The fighting continues in the middle of the street. The man appears calm, but the woman is violently excited, possibly coming down from a drug high. Her shrill voice breaks the night's icy, silent air.

An officer approaches and attempts to subdue the woman while leading her into the wagon. But she fights back—punching, kicking, slapping, anything to break free.

As the scene unfolds, the wagon's light illuminates its major players on a nearby snowbank: the embroiled woman and the arresting officer. Cummins watches their actions in dark shadows, as though he's watching a Hitchcock film: the woman's flying arms, the officer's forearm defense—a surreal scene. Cummins is captivated by the drama and its players. The performance ends with the slam of the wagon's doors, the curtain falling on the makeshift stage.

The facts slowly come to light. The woman is a mother, the aforementioned baby her son, and she threw the baby at the man in her violent rage. The infant rolled under a parked truck before a neighbor rescued him. At the 24th District police station, Cummins has the lady cuffed to the desk and answering questions. Her rage continues and climaxes as her arresting officer approaches. She stands and spits on him. He follows *with a swift kick to her chair, a rattling jar to her insides.*

"Spit on me again," he challenges.

Silence commands the immediate space.

Later, Cummins crosses paths with his fellow officer, who stops Cummins and asks: "Father Cummins, do you think what I did was wrong?"

Cummins takes stock of the question, a seemingly odd inquiry, as if his colleague requests Cummins's approval. "Well, before I give you absolution," says Cummins, "do you think what you did was wrong?"

"Father," the officer answers, "I've got babies of my own."

———————————————★———————————————

"Don't do it, Mr. Cummins. Please don't do it. You'll change. I swear you'll change."

In front of Mike Cummins stood a female student in his senior religion class at St. Ignatius College Prep. Her words laced with fear, concern, and apprehension, she pleaded for Cummins to reconsider—and she did it, to borrow Cummins's words, "with the look of death in her eyes."

In days, Cummins would begin his training for the Chicago Police Department, leaving behind his post as a religion teacher at St. Ignatius, one of the city's most lauded high schools, for the world of law enforcement in the nation's third-largest city. He would also be leaving the stability of teaching behind for the uncertainty of police work, turning his attention to crime and away from academic promise.

"You'll change. You'll be just like him," she said, her words ringing in Cummins's, ears. "Don't do it, Mr. Cummins. Don't do it."

And how was Cummins to answer the pleas of his student, a young girl who doubled as the daughter of a Chicago Police officer? In one academic year, she saw in Cummins what she hadn't seen in her father: an optimism, a hope that the emotion of human acts could be felt. In her own father, she saw the callousness that years on the job inspired, and she didn't want to see Cummins endure the same fate. Her father lost, she reached to save her teacher.

"You'll become just like him," she said again. "Don't do it."

Days before his announcement to students that he would be leaving teaching to pursue a career as a Chicago Police officer, Cummins sat with the

> *Rising beyond gang graffiti, a church steeple reaches into a clear August sky. Chicago Police officer Mike Cummins inhabits both worlds, one of faith and the other of felony.*
> Courtesy of Daniel P. Smith

school's acting principal, Don Nekrosius, a fatherly man with an inquisitive and analytical mind. Upon hearing of Cummins decision, Nekrosius, less concerned with the administrative side of things, asked, "Do you think you could kill someone?" Left to silent contemplation, Cummins wandered in his conscience, considering the question. Could he indeed kill another man if called upon to do so? And now, with this pleading student in front of him, how would he answer her petition—would he change? Would he become "like the rest of them?"

"I still don't know if I could kill somebody, and that's what I told Don Nekrosius when he asked me," Cummins says. "And have I changed? Yes. I feel more cynical. I'm much quicker to judge people on the streets. I can still be shocked and moved, but I see clearly what I should be moved by. But there still exists a moral compulsion to do something to make things right; that has not changed."

Twelve years into the job, Cummins insists that he maintains his spiritual faith and candor in the face of Chicago Police work. While he admits others on the job sometimes appear jaded, he says they, like himself, merely turn off some aspect of their brains to help them cope with all they see. It's merely a survival mechanism, he insists, and a learned human behavior allowing officers to juggle the demands of an unforgiving job with, truth be told, their own sanity. He urges others not to misunderstand.

"People accuse police all the time of being cynical, mean-spirited, quick to judge, and laughing at others' pain. I draw this analogy: it must be difficult for a surgeon to cut someone open, I can't believe it'd be easy. There's something that surgeon must do to turn off something in his soul or spiritual being to not think about the dangerous and delicate situation before him. He wouldn't be able to do his job if he were so sensitive to it," says Cummins.

"An officer has to do things in which he must turn off part of his humanity. He cannot act effectively on emotion. He has to be clearheaded. He needs to discern what went wrong. Who is at fault? How do I control the situation? And that can be confused with crudeness, aggressiveness, and even mean-spiritedness."

Inevitably with Cummins, the question arises: why would you ever leave teaching religion to become a Chicago Police officer? Why move to such a distinct world? Yet, Cummins, who has earned undergraduate and graduate degrees in religious studies, doesn't see the work existing in two separate worlds; his worlds, in fact, overlap.

"People can't see how the worlds fit," he says. "Both are about morality, aren't they? Religious principles and tenets are what define our criminal laws.

"Is it true police do things others see as brutal, profane, quick to judge, and not in line with spiritual morality? Perhaps. But the fact is the police are oftentimes trying to do what's best; they're trying to achieve the general good. We're protecting those who can least protect themselves. We're most obligated to protect those who cannot wait for God's justice to take place."

A self-described academic, Cummins speaks confidently and thoughtfully about his police career, calling upon others' words when necessary—Austrian psychiatrist and author Viktor Frankl, St. Augustine, biblical references. Careful in his details, reflective by nature, and considerate about the issues he faces, Cummins understands the existence of an earthly duty and seeks to fulfill that purpose. This clear outlook has allowed Cummins to create the balance between spiritual faith and police work.

"Ultimately, I believe my spirituality benefits the job because it makes me want to do better, to discover truth as best I can, to do the best I can by victims, not just find the criminal and bring him to justice. Just doing my best reaffirms the victim's faith in the system, in this worldly system that the officer represents."

At 42, Cummins has a youthful look. Clean-cut with short brown curly hair and nary a trace of facial hair, he looks untried, innocent—and in his presence one can find calm and comfort. He speaks softly and his intelligence radiates

> ➤ *With brick and steel warehouses lining much of Lake Street and the Green Line El train screeching overhead, Chicago Police Detective Mike Cummins encountered one of his career's most faithful moments near the intersection of Lake Street and Ashland Avenue. A rape in progress, the victim shook off her attacker, who was later brought to the scene for an immediate identification.*
> Courtesy of Daniel P. Smith

in his recall of details, his historical perspective, and heartfelt opinions. He instructs on the history of the Jesuit priests, reverting to his role as educator as he speaks of a conflict between the Vatican and a small group of Jesuit priests in Central America. The priests, he says, were literally taking up arms to achieve social and political justice.

"It was liberation theology," he says. "Many priests and Christians were working in the here and now. They couldn't wait for God's justice to take place."

At times, Cummins admits to a temptation to join the priesthood, thoughts, he says, more prompted by the Jesuit lifestyle than a "calling." He recalls the Jesuit priests at St. Ignatius taking vows of poverty, yet having access to luxury sedans outside their residence doors.

"I can't say I ever felt called to the priesthood. My study in school was more academic than faith-based. But at times I was tempted to join the priesthood. I thought I could give up this scratch-by-the-way living for a more comfortable lifestyle," says Cummins, who earned the moniker "Father" with his colleagues in the Chicago Police Department given his prior academic and career history.

When Cummins received his graduate degree from St. Louis University, he first attempted to join the St. Louis Police Department but failed the eyesight test. He later found a job as the campus minister at a private high school in Rock

Island, Illinois, in 1987. There, after paying his bills and loans, he retained $90 for the month. With a desire to move to Chicago, Cummins left the Quad Cities in the summer of 1990 and sent his resume to the area's Catholic high schools. He spent one year at all-girls Mother Guerin High School in west suburban River Grove before moving to St. Ignatius in the fall of 1991. After two years at St. Ignatius, Cummins joined the Chicago Police Department at age 30.

"A lot of little kids want to be the police or fire and I was no different," says Cummins, who experienced a nomadic childhood as the son of an Air Force father. "I was always fascinated by the police; I used to love reading detective comic books and stories and watching cop movies."

Cummins's career began Halloween weekend 1993 in Rogers Park, the North Side's 24th District and perhaps the city's most diverse area. He followed that with brief stints at Central Detention at police headquarters and public housing. On Labor Day 2000, Cummins made detective—"the best job in the department," he says. Currently a violent crimes detective, Cummins specifically investigates sex crimes, a position with potentially disheartening findings.

He begins discussing one instance in the summer of 2004, an afternoon on Lake Street near Ashland Avenue, in which he felt his spirituality touch his work. Too often, he says, the police arrive to repair the damage; in rare circumstances, however, Cummins says the most gratifying moments appear from the delivery of immediate justice.

A young lady, recently relocated from Kansas, was walking down Lake Street, the Green Line El train screeching overhead. She saw a man in the distance, but thought little of his presence. When he neared, however, he forced her aside and ripped down her pants. She sent out screams and two men driving by heard her calls, stepping out of their car and moving in. Other bystanders—including the drivers of a Brink's van and a city garbage truck—called 911. The man took off, the police appeared, and both victim and witnesses provided a description of the man. In short time, the man was discovered walking in the area and brought back to the scene where the woman made a positive identification. In this moment, Cummins, a detective responding to the scene, felt this and other bystanders' actions delivered justice, whether defined in the books of Chicago's law or by an ancient moral code.

"I'm so used to being there after the fact. The damage done," says Cummins, a hint of regret in his voice, "it becomes, what can we do to repair the damage?

"There's a central difference between knowing that one has lost and defeating crime. In this instance, we were able to defeat the crime. She is able to go on and live an unimpaired life. I look back at this story with some happiness because she comes out as the winner, the survivor. She screamed and fought and then we got the guy."

With most rape victims, Cummins says he faces the reality that their lives take a different path following the incident. He relies on his faith to reconcile his work and the survivor's life.

"With the rape victims I see as a detective, it's my job to find the attacker and bring him before a judge. It won't repair the damage, but it's the part I can do," he says. "The attacker will be punished in the next life, but I need to know that I did my part to do justice in this world.

"As a religious person, I believe in a higher justice. True, it's not comforting for those victimized in this world, but it's necessary that somebody act as God's justice in this world. That's what police do. Our job is to do the best we can to see that justice is achieved."

As Cummins continues, his sincerity on the topic shines in his words. His police work is grounded in a devout faith. Nevertheless, he maintains a realistic outlook while acknowledging spirituality's high, sometimes uncompromising moral ground.

"For the people who scratch out a tough living—the elderly, the poor, small children—we have to have a system in place to at least make things right for ten minutes. We can't make somebody's life perfect, but we can stop things for a moment," he says. "To a large degree, the police are a quick fix measure."

Not native to Chicago and with most of his life spent in the academic world, Cummins describes himself as an outsider looking in and then entering a world of urban streets where crime has the potential to overshadow all else. He says that before he became a Chicago Police officer, he wouldn't have recognized an unmarked police car, didn't know what a gangway meant. Little made sense to him and he feared he would let his fellow officers down.

"From my first day in the academy I felt like an outsider, like an alien observer," he says. "My eyes were very closed. I was in an academic environment my whole life and then went to a world with very little theory but a lot of practice."

As a police officer, Cummins realizes the penchant for crime to extend its reach, the ability of violence to halt humanity's pulse. He points to the story of Adam and Eve as one that runs parallel with his police work.

"Once Adam and Eve ate from that Tree of Knowledge their eyes opened up," he says. "Prior to that they were innocent, happy, blissful. But once they gave into that temptation, they saw corruption and betrayal.

Like them, my eyes have been opened and I cannot shut them."

Upon leaving his job as a religious educator at St. Ignatius, Cummins penned a personal letter to his students in which he not only offered his gratitude and best hopes, but also provided students a final and continuing assignment. It reads:

1. The salvation of Man is through Love and in Love.
2. There is no Love without Sacrifice.
3. And the third one is up to you, it's your Logos, and it is a fluid and changing thing. The only thing I know for certain is that if it flows logically from the first two, you'll be all right, and that is my prayer for you. Feel free to forget anything else that you may have accidentally learned. Live for that.

The letter concluded, "I hope we'll all discover that, each in our own way, we are building up the Kingdom of God here on earth, just as it is in heaven. Let's let that be sufficient unto the day."

As Mike Cummins discovered his footing as well as the proper perspective, he goes about his work with the Chicago Police Department in the same way he lives out his faith—in electing to work for the positive in the face of consistent adversity.

"You get what you're willing to work for," he says. "There's so much will to do what you want—it's a human spirituality. The last freedom we have is to choose our way in given situations.

"I don't always have spiritual values in the forefront of my mind. Sometimes the cynicism, the professional jargon takes over. There's a central difficulty for most spiritual people to keep their values in mind during a given situation, but maybe it's easier for the police because there is a moral black and white in so many situations. There is a victim and there is a criminal; there is a right and there is a wrong."

Understanding a sometimes cynical public's perception of his work, Cummins believes his work maintains value; still, he also admits that the job takes a piece of the self—a worthy sacrifice in his mind.

"I believe what I do as a Chicago Police officer is important; it's work that has to be done," he says. "Maybe I do have to sacrifice some—my innocence, my trustfulness—to do the job well. But I realize it's a sacrifice for the betterment of the community and individuals. Ultimately, I know I'm doing my part."

MEANINGFUL WORK:
FATHER TOM NANGLE, CPD CHAPLAIN

———————————————————★———————————————————

The date is Sunday, September 11, 2005, and it's a somber time for many across the nation. At the Mercy Home Chapel, immediately west of Chicago's Loop, Father Tom Nangle presides over a Catholic mass to an intimate gathering of 40 or so, all of them connected in some way to the Chicago Police Department.

Given the trauma Hurricane Katrina dispelled across the Gulf Coast only days before, in addition to the historical significance of September 11, Father Nangle's mass takes on an even more reflective, insightful tone.

"In the last couple of days," Nangle says of the disaster in New Orleans, "we've seen people capable of the most horrible acts of human nature and the most magnificent acts of human nature. And then I stopped and thought, 'You know, this is what coppers see each day.'"

With that opening comment, Nangle begins mass. Chicago Police Superintendent Phil Cline shares the opening readings and Nangle follows with a brief gospel. His homily begins with an admission of struggle.

"I didn't quite know what I would say today," says Nangle, a man who rarely strains to find words. "I thought I might ask you how you felt on 9/11. But I know how you felt—angry, afraid, confused. And then I said, 'There's Nangle at his brightest thinking. Ask 'em what you already know.'" Nangle's own chuckle accompanies the guests' laughter.

"But each time we suffer," Nangle continues, "our soul is reshaped. And I thought I would ask all of you today where your soul is today as you think of what happened four years ago or what just happened down in the Gulf Coast—what's in your soul today?"

The invitation for dialogue extended, a few officers lend their words. One talks of waning patriotism, the run on American flags that dominated the immediate post-9/11 America, now replaced with curious looks from passersby each time he raises the flag at his home.

"Each day, I see fewer and fewer American flags flying," he says.

Another speaks of white marble gates at the United States–Canadian border.

"It's a sad day that those gates have to be closed, because it's not what this country's about," he says.

In the back row, an older officer speaks of fear.

"I don't know if we're prepared to handle another attack—and the terrorists just saw that, the whole world just saw that," he offers.

At one point in the mass, Father Nangle asks an officer to stand and share an excerpt from a recent Chicago newspaper article. The story tells of a group of Chicago officers traveling to New Orleans to provide help following Hurricane Katrina's devastation. She unfolds the article and begins reading. The story recounts a New Orleans man, in a heated discussion with a local officer, pointing to a Chicago cop and saying, "The real police are here."

The chapel fills with applause. Alongside the burdens of life, many of the chapel's inhabitants are reminded of their dual citizenship—they are human beings with very human emotions and yet also Chicago Police officers, the objective beings relied upon to be rational—and even heroic—leaders in chaotic times.

And that dual citizenship, the often-tenuous residence amid what duty demands and what humanity feels, cannot be easy. Today, this much is clear.

———————————————★———————————————

In 1970, Tom Nangle was a young priest immediately out of the seminary. Sent to a South Side parish where he knew no one, the native West and North Sider traveled to a backyard barbecue to begin meeting members of his new congregation.

During the barbecue a long Dodge pulled up and a pair of men exited the vehicle. With handguns peering from their sides, the men walked through the gathering, shaking hands, wandering over to the food table, and eventually finding themselves in conversation with Nangle. Later, one would suggest to the rookie priest, "If you really want to meet your neighbors, then come with us."

Nangle accepted the offer from John Thulis and Ron Spivak, a pair of tactical officers from Chicago's Sixth District, and the proposal changed the course of Nangle's life. It was not his first ride-along (he had joined a former high school classmate in 1965 back when, he says, "The police were even more unpopular"), but it was the first time in his life he experienced a sincere interest in police work. For the next ten years, Nangle traveled the neighborhood's streets three nights a week with Thulis, Spivak, and others on the unit's tactical team. While he did meet his neighbors, he also came to recognize the many layers of Chicago Police work—in the most truthful and real of circumstances.

"I loved the excitement, but more, the substantial nature of the work I saw," says Nangle, a gray-haired 61-year-old who sports a thick black mustache, round glasses, and piercing wit. "I learned how substantial and awe-filled some moments are in an officer's life. I saw work with a spiritual, Godly dimension to it that I had never heard anybody talk about. I saw them take guns off the street, arrest rapists and robbers, and get drug busts."

After ten years at his South Side parish and his weekly shadowing of

➤ *Chicago Police Department Chaplain Father Tom Nangle poses with Chicago Police officers (from left) Mike D'Andrea and his partner, John O'Shea, just moments before the Chicago Bulls clinch their fourth NBA title and celebratory Chicagoans pour into the streets.*
Courtesy of John O'Shea

officers, Nangle was appointed Chicago Police Department chaplain, a post he has held for the last 25 years.

"When I started this job, I thought if nothing else. I wanted to remind officers that their job was sacred, noble, and worthy," says Nangle. "I wanted them to know that there are moments in their day that God notices."

His daily work with officers and footing in the Chicago Police culture provides him insight that few outsiders ever achieve. Firsthand, often alongside officers, Nangle encounters the range of Chicago's social ills—from domestic violence to gang warfare, from drug trafficking to murder and everything in between.

"This is a world filled with unspeakable horror, cruelty, and suffering," says Nangle. The Chicago Police are almost always called to the scene of that. I sometimes wonder if their souls don't get saturated with that. They see so much horror and human suffering; you wonder how they can go on."

There is a ministry aspect to police work, says Nangle. The best police officers are often guided by an intrinsic motivation as well as a high sense of honor and duty. This cannot be ignored.

"You'll find that the best Chicago officers do it because they're the police and because it's the right thing to do; they don't care so much about medals. My job has never been a desk or office job. It's to spend time in the middle of it all. That's where the fun, heroism, and horror all exist. You know, I get to see the magnificent things the Chicago cops do and I'm reminded that it's one of the few jobs in America in which heroism is expected. But then that heroism is not often recognized or noted. One of my great aches—and this is something I've had now for 35 years—is that the Chicago Police are not understood. They're not appreciated by citizens or the media. I've seen Chicago cops do things that are heroic, sacred, and generous—over and over and all in one day. Yet, too often, that's not how we view them."

Stopping to drink some coffee from a white Styrofoam cup, Nangle glances at a table across the Mercy Home cafeteria. There sits a group of officers and their spouses, chatting away on a post-mass Sunday afternoon. Nangle looks younger than his 61 years; despite the fleeting hair, a grin seems inherent on his face. His insight reflects the balance of intellectual wisdom and street smarts. With the ability to call upon either, he mixes splashes of humor and wit with dashes of philosophy and theory. Most often, his speech is direct, yet soft and unthreatening. Though he may ramble and stumble over thoughts, he always arrives at his point. He places his coffee cup down.

"And another thing," he says, "the police are the last group in America that intelligent people still feel free to be prejudiced against. They're stereotyped by some of the most intelligent people I know. When that line of thought starts, I just walk away. It won't be a conversation."

Nangle begins discussing the case of a three-year-old girl riding her big wheel in an alley. Caught amid gang crossfire, the young girl died.

"I stopped in the area and saw the energy and competency of the detectives. I went out on the street to see the squads and tact cars on a mission to solve this," he says. "And they got the shooters.

"The whole time, though, some people in the community were saying, 'Where were the police?' They misplaced, displaced—whatever you want to call it—their anger on the police. Nobody in the city really saw the intensity, competency, and hard work that went into solving that murder. The police were just the lightning rod for criticism. It makes my heart ache because I know how good they are. I know what they pour into their work.

"I don't know how many times I've seen a fatal shooting and the hours, diligence, and street wisdom the Chicago coppers bring to the equation. Sometimes you wonder if anybody thanks them, if anybody even notices when they do a good job."

If no one else does, then certainly Nangle notices the work—labeling it with such words as "worthy" and "sacred." What's more, he's come to understand a group of individuals passionate and committed to their work. Certainly not all, he'll admit, but a deep corps of honorable and courageous folk. In riding around with Spivak, Thulis, and other Sixth District officers, Nangle recalls conversations discussing the Church and organized religion, his own world, itself the subject of criticism. "Organized religion didn't always hold much for them," he says. "But to a person, they believed in God, right and wrong, and justice. That's what drove them."

Nangle breaks away to share good-byes with a group of officers and their spouses, sharing firm handshakes and kisses on the cheek. Updated on the status of some officers battling their own struggles, Nangle returns to offer more insight.

"Not a week goes by that I don't hear an officer say, 'You know, Father, you won't believe it, but I pray every day.' And I do believe it. Being the police, seeing what they see, it either intensifies your relationship with your creator or diminishes it," says Nangle.

Two weeks ago, as he stood washing his breakfast dishes in his North Side apartment, Nangle looked out the window at a bright summer morning, and happened upon as clear a thought as he had experienced in weeks.

"I prayed and thanked God that my work has meaning. It's work that feeds my soul. What a great thing I have because all of us want meaningful work and I have it."

Out of his pocket Nangle pulls his Chicago Police star, one he's carried for over two dozen years, and runs his fingers over it—up, down, and across.

"Look at this," he says, "it's fading."

Closing the black leather flap that guards the star, he taps its top with his knuckles and returns the star to his pocket. He stands and says, "I gotta run. Got things to do."

And away he walks.

More meaningful work. For himself and for others.

LAST CALL

For a metropolitan city, Chicago's as close as you may get to small-town, Main Street America. I rediscovered that each time I sat to talk with an officer. Everybody knew everybody and a common ground could always be established, often extending deep into personal lives.

Mike Cummins worked in Area Four with John O'Shea, who has known my Uncle John for over 30 years. Joe Barnes is a sergeant in Special Operations, where one of his soldiers was Miguel Rios. Rick King worked in the Canine Unit with Bob Rawa (or "Bobby," as colleague Joe Barnes calls him).

Art Hannus's grandfather was murdered, as was C.K. Rojas's. George Salituro's son, Chris, was a teacher of mine at St. Patrick High School; Sal also worked at O'Hare with Willie Calabrese. Dave Kumiega was my brother's partner in the 25th District, where Bryan Spreng, who went through the police academy with C.K. Rojas, now works. Bill Jaconetti, who once called John O'Shea's neighbor Joe DeLopez boss, hosts a radio show on a local AM station called "Cop Talk" and has had John Folino Jr. on as a guest. Jim Rohrlack's wife is a fondly

➤ Courtesy of Jennifer Sisson Photography

➤ Courtesy of Jennifer Sisson Photography

remembered elementary school teacher of mine. Beth Russell frequently attends mass presided over by Chaplain Tom Nangle, a spirited fellow with too many connections to list. Cindy Pontoriero referred to my late uncle Joe Mahoney as a "second father."

And the list goes on. The common ground established, we Chicagoans forge ahead in honest dialogue about our city and our lives. Now I am linked to these men and women; they're a part of my life as much as I'm a part of theirs. We have our own bonds, our own link to add in the six-degrees-of-separation game, as well as the ink-and-paper history to prove our relationship.

I love this city and refuse to conceal that emotion. We are a city built on spirit, resilience, and passion. And at the center of this city are the people. In this book we meet people, hear their stories, and peer into their lives—and in so doing, we peer into the world of the Chicago Police Department as well. But first, we see the police officers as individuals working their way through life's journey as spouses, parents, spiritual beings, dreamers and idealists, realists and cynics. They are our neighbors and friends, as complex and ordinary as any of us. Our ability to understand them, to empathize, will only help us all create a more unified city, a true "pencil town" moving ahead to our next glorious steps.

After months of work, *On the Job* reached the goal it set (at least in the intentions of my young mind): to offer readers a glimpse into the soul of the Chicago Police Department and activate an understanding of the officers' lives and work. We saw Chicago's officers wrestle with decisions, relish their work, and share with us their own fears and apprehensions. We met those who still battle with the aftereffects of firing their guns; we observed officers committed to pursuing a long-held dream; we heard people discuss wanting to make our city a better place; and we observed officers transferring the talk into action. Admittedly, they all have faults. But let there be no mistake, Chicago is blessed to claim such individuals— those who help make Chicago what it is and what it will become.

And as Mike Cummins said, "Let's let that be sufficient unto the day."

ENDNOTES

PART 1
THE CHICAGO WAY: POLICE WORK IN THE URBAN LANDSCAPE

1. Andrea Seligman, "Crime and Chicago's Image," *Encyclopedia of Chicago,* (Chicago: Univ. of Chicago Press, 2004), 218-221.

2. Christopher Thale, "Haymarket and May Day," *Encyclopedia of Chicago,* (Chicago: Univ. of Chicago Press, 2004), 375-376.

3. John J. Flinn, *History of the Chicago Police,* (Montclair, NJ: Patterson Smith, 1973), xix.

4. Richard Lindberg, *To Serve and Collect: Chicago Politics and Police Corruption from the Lager Beer Riot to the Summerdale Scandal,* (New York: Praeger, 1991), 108.

5. Andrew J. Diamond, "Gangs," *Encyclopedia of Chicago,* (Chicago: Univ. of Chicago Press, 2004), 324.

6. Nelson Algren, *Chicago: City on the Make,* (Chicago: Univ. of Chicago Press, 2001), 21.

7. Richard Whittingham, *Joe D: On the Street with a Chicago Homicide Cop,* (Niles, IL: Argus Communications, 1980), 33.

8. Nelson Algren, *Chicago: City on the Make,* (Chicago: Univ. of Chicago Press, 2001), 23.

9. Nelson Algren, *Chicago: City on the Make,* (Chicago: Univ. of Chicago Press, 2001), 14.

10. "Murder and the wave machine," *Chicago Tribune,* 4 July 2004.

11. Chicago Police Department 2004 annual report.

12. Frank Kusch, *Battleground Chicago: the Police and the 1968 Democratic National Convention,* (Westport, CT: Praeger, 2004), 122.

13. Gina Gallo, *Armed and Dangerous: Memoirs of a Chicago Policewoman,* (New York: Forge, 2001), 15.

14. Nelson Algren, *Chicago: City on the Make,* (Chicago: Univ. of Chicago Press, 2001), 68.

PART 2
TRAVELS: THE JOURNEY OF THE CHICAGO POLICE

1. Leeds, Patricia, "What do stars mean to cops? Here's answer," *Chicago Tribune,* 19 March 1950.

2. Leeds, Patricia, "What do stars mean to cops? Here's answer," *Chicago Tribune,* 19 March 1950.

3. Christopher Thale, "Police," *Encyclopedia of Chicago,* (Chicago: Univ. of Chicago Press, 2004), 626.

4. Richard Lindberg, *To Serve and Collect: Chicago Politics and Police Corruption from the Lager Beer Riot to the Summerdale Scandal,* (New York: Praeger, 1991), 5.

5. Richard Lindberg, *To Serve and Collect: Chicago Politics and Police Corruption from the Lager Beer Riot to the Summerdale Scandal,* (New York: Praeger, 1991), 15.

6. Richard Lindberg, *To Serve and Collect: Chicago Politics and Police Corruption from the Lager Beer Riot to the Summerdale Scandal,* (New York: Praeger, 1991), 24.

7. Richard Lindberg, *To Serve and Collect: Chicago Politics and Police Corruption from the Lager Beer Riot to the Summerdale Scandal,* (New York:

Praeger, 1991), 15, 51-52.

8. Richard Lindberg, *To Serve and Collect: Chicago Politics and Police Corruption from the Lager Beer Riot to the Summerdale Scandal,* (New York: Praeger, 1991), xi.

9. Richard Lindberg, *To Serve and Collect: Chicago Politics and Police Corruption from the Lager Beer Riot to the Summerdale Scandal,* (New York: Praeger, 1991), 111.

10. Citizen's Police Committee (Chicago), *Chicago Police Problems,* (Montclair, NJ: Patterson Smith, 1969), 46.

11. Richard Lindberg, *To Serve and Collect: Chicago Politics and Police Corruption from the Lager Beer Riot to the Summerdale Scandal,* (New York: Praeger, 1991), 213.

12. Citizen's Police Committee (Chicago), *Chicago Police Problems,* (Montclair, NJ: Patterson Smith, 1969), 229, 250-252.

13. Chicago Public Library's "Brief History of the Chicago Police Department."

14. Richard Lindberg, *To Serve and Collect: Chicago Politics and Police Corruption from the Lager Beer Riot to the Summerdale Scandal,* (New York: Praeger, 1991), 294.

15. Richard Lindberg, *To Serve and Collect: Chicago Politics and Police Corruption from the Lager Beer Riot to the Summerdale Scandal,* (New York: Praeger, 1991), 307.

16. Bernie Mixon, "Englewood shows cops gratitude," *Chicago Tribune,* 23 Oct 1994.

17. Ray Quintanilla, "City beat patrols a year old and learning how to walk," *Chicago Tribune,* 20 May 1994.

18. "The Summer Killing Season," *Chicago Tribune,* 2 May 2004.

19. "Chicago Police release revised '04 murder tally," *Chicago Tribune,* 23 Jan 2005.

20. Robert Blau, *The Cop Shop: True Crime on the Streets of Chicago,* (Reading, MA: Addison-Wesley Publishing Co., 1993), 61.

"EVOLUTION"
—JOHN O'SHEA

1. David Farber, *Chicago '68*, (Chicago: University of Chicago Press, 1988).

"UNCLE WILLIE"
—WILLIAM CALABRESE

1. William Recktenwald, "Nearly 70, Chicago police officer not the least bit eager to hang it up," *Chicago Tribune*, 19 Feb 1990.

PART 3
WHO ARE WE?
ORGANIZATION AND
CULTURE OF THE
CHICAGO POLICE
DEPARTMENT

1. Connie Fletcher, *What Cops Know: Cops Talk about What They Do, How They Do It, and What It Does to Them*, (New York: Pocket Books, 1992), xii.

2. Richard Lindberg, *To Serve and Collect: Chicago Politics and Police Corruption from the Lager Beer Riot to the Summerdale Scandal*, (New York: Praeger, 1991).

3. Connie Fletcher, *What Cops Know: Cops Talk about What They Do,*

How They Do It, and What It Does to Them, (New York: Pocket Books, 1992), 5, 18.

4. Robert Blau, *The Cop Shop: True Crime on the Streets of Chicago*, (Reading, MA: Addison-Wesley Publishing Co., 1993), 115.

5. Wesley G. Skogan and Susan M. Hartnett, *Community Policing, Chicago Style*, (New York: Oxford Univ. Press, 1997), 78.

6. Robert Blau, *The Cop Shop: True Crime on the Streets of Chicago*, (Reading, MA: Addison-Wesley Publishing Co., 1993), 49.

7. Chicago Police Department 2004 annual report.

PART 4
POLICE WORK, THE
PERSON, THE LIFE, AND
THE SPIRIT

1. L.H. Whittemore, *Cop! A Closeup of Violence and Tragedy*, (New York: Holt, Reinhart, & Winston, 1969), 192.

2. Gina Gallo, *Armed and Dangerous: Memoirs of a Chicago Policewoman*, (New York: Forge,

2001), 214.

3. Richard Lindberg, *To Serve and Collect: Chicago Politics and Police Corruption from the Lager Beer Riot to the Summerdale Scandal*, (New York: Praeger, 1991), xv.

4. Gina Gallo, *Armed and Dangerous: Memoirs of a Chicago Policewoman*, (New York: Forge, 2001), 98.

5. Richard Lindberg, *To Serve and Collect: Chicago Politics and Police Corruption from the Lager Beer Riot to the Summerdale Scandal*, (New York: Praeger, 1991), 36.

6. Citizen's Police Committee (Chicago), *Chicago Police Problems*, (Montclair, NJ: Patterson Smith, 1969), 7, 17.

7. Citizen's Police Committee (Chicago), *Chicago Police Problems*, (Montclair, NJ: Patterson Smith, 1969), 6.

8. Citizen's Police Committee (Chicago), *Chicago Police Problems*, (Montclair, NJ: Patterson Smith, 1969), 37-8.

9. Richard Lindberg,
*To Serve and Collect:
Chicago Politics and
Police Corruption from
the Lager Beer Riot
to the Summerdale
Scandal,* (New York:
Praeger, 1991), 53.

10. Jack Muller, *I, Pig; or,
How the World's Most
Famous Cop, Me, Is
Fighting City Hall,*
(New York: Morrow,
1971), 129.

11. Jack Muller, *I, Pig; or,
How the World's Most
Famous Cop, Me, Is
Fighting City Hall,*
(New York: Morrow,
1971), 132-3.

12. Jack Muller, *I, Pig; or,
How the World's Most
Famous Cop, Me, Is
Fighting City Hall,*
(New York: Morrow,
1971), 153.

13. W.H. Kroes, B.L.
Margolis, & J.J.
Hurrell, Jr., "Job Stress
in Policemen," *Journal
of Police Science and
Administration,* 2
(1974), 145-155.

14. Robert Blau, *The Cop
Shop: True Crime
on the Streets of
Chicago,* (Reading,
MA: Addison-Wesley
Publishing Co., 1993),
180.

15. "Drug Use by Cops
Seen as Growing
Problem," *Law
Enforcement News,* 23
Sept 1985, 1,12.

16. Roy R. Roberg and
Jack Kuykendall,
Police and Society,
(Belmont, CA:
Wadsworth, 1993),
427.

17. Gina Gallo, *Armed
and Dangerous:
Memoirs of a Chicago
Policewoman,* (New
York: Forge, 2001),
326.

INDEX

ACKNOWLEDGMENTS

O*n the Job* is not my endeavor alone. Though the cover bears my name, the journey to publication was one I shared with many fellow Chicagoans who provided doses of support, encouragement, time, energy, feedback, sincerity, and guidance.

I am first indebted to Lake Claremont Press, publisher Sharon Woodhouse, assistant publisher Elizabeth Sattelberger, editors Barbara Hughett and Diana Solomon, cover designer Timothy Kocher, and designer Patti Corcoran. In our first discussion, I told Sharon I wanted to publish *On the Job* with a Chicago company, someone sharing my passion for this city; I am grateful that Sharon saw promise in this project, committed her resources to pulling it off, and afforded me the spectacular opportunity to add to this city's rich dialogue. For a Chicago kid, nothing could be better.

To capture the soul of Chicago's officers, I first needed coppers willing to candidly discuss the work-life juxtaposition, scarcely an easy feat given law enforcement's general distrust of the media. Still, many officers allowed me into their world, sharing time and stories with clarity and purpose. Deep thanks belong to the officers whose stories line these pages: Brian Spreng, Dave Kumiega, Miguel Rios, C.K. Rojas, Art Hannus, John O'Shea, Bill Jaconetti, Joe DeLopez, William Calabrese, Cindy Pontoriero, Rick King, George Salituro, Bob Rawa, John Folino Jr., Beth Russell, Jim Rohrlack, Joe Barnes Jr., Mike Cummins, and Father Tom Nangle.

Many others provided a helpful lead, a heads-up phone call, or their own insight and skills to push this project along, including Rory Gilbert, Marty Philbin, John McIntyre, Bobby Smith, John Folino Sr., Chris

Salituro, Nick Schuler, Richard Ressman, Michael Mazek, Jim Knoedel, Jim Montes, Mark Indreika, Rhonda Anderson, Kevin Smith of the Chicago Police Department's Office of Emergency Management, Chicago Police Sergeant Kristin Barker, retired CPD James T. McGuire, Teresa Yoder of the Chicago Public Library, Rich Lindberg, Frank Kusch, my audio/visual guru, Joey Bicicchi, and, my favorite freelance photographer, Jennifer Sisson.

There are a few whose impact merits additional mention: Dr. Gabriele Rico, whose guidance continues from 2,000 miles away; Bob Davis, whose spirit remains, though he is in the heavens; Dennis Witt, who told me to be a writer; and Don Nekrosius, who understands the soul of at least this young man.

As writers, we are often infected with the spirits of those we most admire, those whose pens dance across the page and entice us all with the power of story. I owe special thanks to those unique talents who have provided the template and inspired me to ascend: Mike Royko, Studs Terkel, Mitch Albom, Robert Fulghum, Antoine de Saint-Exupery, and Rick Kogan, a fellow Lake Claremont Press author and one of Chicago's last real newspapermen.

And, finally, such a list cannot conclude without praise to those who have supported and encouraged this project as well as my young career: Mary Ellen Smith, who knows true sacrifice; Tina Smith, as lovely a wife as lovely can be; Mary Helen McIntyre; William Mahoney; Bobby, April, Sarah, and RJ Smith; Michele, Tony, Alyssa, and Amanda Lendino; the McIntyre, Keehnast, Sloan, and Mahoney families; the Lazzara family; Shawn Sullivan; Russ Riberto; Joe Marren; Tristan Roche; Graham Waller; Dave Johnson; June Oliva; Nick Pasturczak; the Walsh family; Dr. Joseph Schmidt and St. Patrick High School; Coach; the late Max Kurland; Wayne Haworth and Dick Pond Athletics; Greg Houghton, Jennifer Mifflin, Suzanne DeChatelet, and Rex Robinson; Ann Gossy, Jeff Rodengen, and Write Stuff Books; and my former students at both St. Ignatius College Prep and Downers Grove South High School. *On the Job* beats with your pulse as well.

ABOUT THE AUTHOR

Already an award-winning, nationally published journalist, Daniel P. Smith left his second career as a high school English teacher behind in 2004 to pursue the writing life. Less than five months removed from the classroom and 23 years old, Smith teamed with Chicago-based Lake Claremont Press to write *On the Job: Behind the Stars of the Chicago Police Department,* inspired by his roots in a Chicago Police family. He is presently working with photographer and fellow Chicagoan Brian Palm on a project sharing the stories and images of Chicago's disappearing buildings. A 2003 graduate of the University of Illinois at Chicago, where he was an accomplished track and field athlete, Smith lives in the city's western suburbs with his wife, Tina, and dog, Dublin. He resides in cyberspace at onthejob-smith.blogspot.com.

LAKE CLAREMONT PRESS

Founded in 1994, Lake Claremont Press specializes in books on the Chicago area and its history, focusing on preserving the city's past, exploring its present environment, and cultivating a strong sense of place for the future. Visit us on the Web at *www.lakeclaremont.com*.

SELECTED BOOKLIST

Great Chicago Fires: Historic Blazes That Shaped a City

The Firefighter's Best Friend: Lives and Legends of Chicago Firehouse Dogs

Chicago TV Horror Movie Shows: From Shock Theatre to Svengoolie

The Golden Age of Chicago Children's Television

A Chicago Tavern: A Goat, a Curse, and the American Dream

Wrigley Field's Last World Series: The Wartime Chicago Cubs and the Pennant of 1945

Chicago's Midway Airport: The First Seventy-Five Years

Today's Chicago Blues

The Chicago River Architecture Tour

Graveyards of Chicago: The People, History, Art, and Lore of Cook County Cemeteries

Chicago Haunts: Ghostlore of the Windy City

More Chicago Haunts: Scenes from Myth and Memory

Award-winners

The Streets & San Man's Guide to Chicago Eats

A Cook's Guide to Chicago

The Chicago River: A Natural and Unnatural History

Near West Side Stories: Struggles for Community in Chicago's Maxwell Street Neighborhood

Finding Your Chicago Ancestors: A Beginner's Guide to Family History in the City and Cook County

The Politics of Place: A History of Zoning in Chicago

Coming Soon

Rule 53: Capturing Hippies, Spies, Politicians, and Murderers in an American Courtroom

From Lumber Hookers to the Hooligan Fleet: A Treasury of Chicago Maritime History

For Members Only: A History and Guide to Chicago's Oldest Private Clubs

Oldest Chicago

Food, Lodging, Liquor: Signs You're in Chicago

Voices from an October City: The Best of Chicago Haunts (audiobook)

Finding Your Chicago Irish

The SportsTraveler's Fanbook to Chicago

Carless in Chicago

Chicago Haunts 3: From the Secret Files of Chicago Hauntings, Inc.